Vintage Verse

James Ball Naylor

Vintage Verse

by

James Ball Naylor

edited & annotated by

Theresa Marie Flaherty

TURAS PUBLISHING

www.TurasPublishing.com

Vintage Verse
by James Ball Naylor
edited and annotated by Theresa Marie Flaherty

10 9 8 7 6 5 4 3 2 1

ISBN-13: 978-0-9832342-8-9

Cover Design: Michael Flaherty
Cover Photo courtesy of Jean Naylor Finley - Naylor Family, 1913: Anne, Mrs. Naylor, Lucile, Dr. Naylor, Lena, Jean, Olive, and Robert.
Back Cover Photo of Naylor entertaining courtesy of Greg and Ellen Hill.
Photo of James Ball Naylor courtesy of the Morgan County Historical Society.
Photo of Lucile Naylor courtesy of Greg & Ellen Hill.
Bookplate courtesy of Robert Naylor.
Photo of Naylor with his Studebacker Commander courtesy of Greg & Ellen Hill.
Poems used with permission of Lucile Naylor and Jean Naylor Finley.

TURAS
PUBLISHING
www.TurasPublishing.com

Lucile's Tribute
to Daddie

Table of Contents

Tribute Series

Vintage Verse is the first book
in a tribute series to
James Ball Naylor.

TURAS
PUBLISHING

Introduction

James Ball Naylor was one of the most well known authors in the country at the turn of the twentieth century, but he faded into the shadows of obscurity after a lifetime of literary work that included eight novels, three children's books, numerous short stories, and six volumes of collected verse. One of his novels—Ralph Marlowe was a best seller in 1901.

It was in poetry—his first love, however, that he discovered his talent for expressing emotions and painting word pictures that appealed to readers. Long before his first two volumes of poetry—Current Coins Picked Up at a Railway Station and Golden Rod and Thistle Down, were published, Naylor's poems appeared in local and national newspapers and magazines.

From the earliest appearance of his poems in print, the public received them enthusiastically, and he was frequently asked to recite them. No one could deliver his lines the way he did with exactly the right rhythm and emphasis. Already known as a gifted speaker in political circles, before long he was an exceptional entertainer and platform speaker on the Lyceum and Chautauqua circuits that brought culture and education to the public long before the era of radio, movies, and television. Naylor brought his poetry to life for his audiences who often responded with standing ovations.

In this volume are poems that Naylor's daughter, Lucile, culled from her collection of family treasures and scrapbooks in an effort to preserve these poems as a tribute to her father. Working with my own mentor, D. W. Garber, an Ohio historian, she meticulously copied nearly one hundred poems in her beautiful Spencerian handwriting, as well as the additional pages required to complete a book—title page, preface, and index that they hoped to have published. The title of this one-of-kind bound volume is The Second Book of Vagrant Verse. This treasure was passed to me by Garber and is the source for most of this volume.

Garber's interest in Naylor began as a very young boy when he met Dr. Naylor, who was a friend of his father's. From that point on, for more than fifty years, he collected everything he could find on Naylor. This collection, one that I have added to over the past thirty years, plus extensive research provided the basis for my book, The Final Test - A Biography of James Ball Naylor

As Naylor's biographer, I catalogued and copied every poem of his that I encountered. These number over eight hundred poems. Only a little over three hundred appear in his collected works. This volume increases the number by about a hundred more. Amazingly that leaves nearly half of his poems that currently are not available to the public.

Theresa Marie Flaherty

Nettie Lucile Naylor

Photo courtesy of Greg & Ellen Hill.

Preface

I, the second child of James Ball Naylor, am making the effort to preserve all those poems of Father's not included in any of his published volumes of verse.

Thus copied, by me, longhand, from old and deteriorating scrapbooks of mine, I trust that you, dear reader, will be lenient in your critical view of these copies of them.

All but one of them have been published in newspapers--local, state, and national, or in magazines. They date all the way from the late 1880s to 1945——the year of his death.

The name S.Q. Lapius was Father's nom de plume--or pseudonym——and was used only in the very early days of his writing, thus dating some of the poems herein recorded.

Father used to say that poetry must have "rhyme, rhythm, and sense," but one will note that he added a bit of nonsense now and then.

Lucile Naylor
Feb. 20, 1968

Vintage Verse

Lucile

She's a dainty little maiden,
    Is Lucile;
And her eyes, with sunshine laden,
    Make me feel
That I can't resist her charms,
But must take her in my arms,
And my wounded heart with countless kisses heal.

Oh, her face is like the flowers
    In the spring;
And her breath's the fragrant showers
    That they fling
To the breezes of the June,
When the wild birds are in tune,
And the woodlands far and wide with music ring.

She's the sweetest little fairy
    That I know;
But she's rather small to marry,
    Yet she'll grow.
I would ask her mama, maybe,
For her darling year-old baby,
But I fear she'd think her young to have a beau.

by S. Q. Lapius (1892)

. . . . . .

Along the Road Called Yesterday

Along the road called Yesterday!—
    A patter in the dust and heat!—
There come to me from far away
    A pair of tiny feet.

Two tiny tired feet that bear
    A slender form, a little lad
Of sunburnt face and tousled hair—
    And sometimes good, and sometimes bad.

I know him—and I know him well;
    His sturdy limbs, his movements free,
His voice the tinkle of a bell—
    The little lad I used to be.

He says, a twinkle in his eyes—
    The while he looks me through and through:
"To think, ah me! That you were I!
    To think, alas, that I am you!"

He turns aside, he heaves a sigh—
    A breath of disillusionment!—
And walks away; and I—and I—
    I gaze along the road he went!

by James Ball Naylor

. . . . . .

True Friendship

True friendship doesn't consist of sweet
  Beatitudes of speech;
Nor does it consist of phrases neat—
  And the platitudes they preach.
It's the helping hand that lifts the load
  From tired shoulders weighted down;
And the hearty smile that smoothes the road
  For bruised feet bare and brown,
It's a word of fellowship and cheer—
  Just the homely word and kind!—
That falling upon the pain-dulled ear
  Brings peace to the tortured mind.
Yea, friendship is naught but a hearty smile,--
  A spring in a desert land—
And a word of cheer just once in a while,
  And the brawn of a helping hand.

by James Ball Naylor

. . . . . .

A Peep Into the Medical Future

- 1894 -

Worthy comrades in medicine, hearken, I pray,
I've a wonderful story to tell you today—
A story o'er-brimming with wisdom and wit,
And having a time-honored moral to it—
A marveleous vision to bring to your view,
Nothing more, nothing less, than a peep at the new
Things that medical science is holding in store,
For nineteen-hundred and ninety-four.

We must look to the future for courage and light,
For the past is enwrapped in the blackness of night;
We must press toward the future for comfort and aid,
For the past is bestrewed with the blunders we've made.
Yet this thought lends us solace and calms all our fears;
Our well-beloved science keeps pace with the years;
And a hundred years hence, will present an array
That will frighten grim Death from his banquet away.

In a hundred years more, at our present mad pace,
With the secrets of life we will stand face to face;
Will discover the soul in some cerebral nook,
And will read a man's mind as we now read a book.
The most hidden diseases we'll readily find—
For we'll diagnose cases by scanning the mind—
And discover their seat in abdomen or chest,
Just like—"You touch the button and we do the rest!"

Yes, we'll search out the way to a true diagnosis—
Differentiate love from a case of chlorosis—
And in prognosis be so extremely exact,
That the papers will always record as a fact;
"John Smith is no more; for the doctor has said
That at 9:24 he will surely be dead,
And the worthy physician has carefully reckoned
The time he will live to the part of a second!"

Why, we'll call on a patient, we'll look at his tongue
And remark: "My dear sir, I must tell you, your lung
Is in such a condition—I'm sorry to say
That your life will go out in a week from today.
Make your piece, my good man, call your relatives in
And apportion to each his allotment of tin;
Trim your sails to embark for eternity's shore."
And they'll carve on his headstone the date—"'94."

We'll record every cough, we'll record every laugh—
Every sneeze—every groan—in a big phonograph;
And we'll keep a true record by filing away
The separate cylinders day after day.
And young Fweddy Van Jones will come 'round on the sly.
"Just to heal, doncher know, what a love of a cry
He had when a baby." We'll make out our fee—
And send the bill in to his governor—See?

As to surgery——mystic and magic art!
In a century more, we'll take out the heart;
And insert a machine for the blood's circulation,
That will run without losing a single pulsation;
And by moving the hand on the dial, you know,
The happy contrivance will run fast or slow.
A proposal of marriage;——who'll dread to begin it,
When his heart will not beat at two hundred a minute?

Oh! the women, dear souls, if deceived by the men,
Will not dare to hint of their broken hearts then;
Or some chivalrous doctor will offer himself
To each one——with a cart-load of hearts from his shelf——
And insist on replacing the one she has lost,
With a newer and better, at nominal cost.
The black-art will be naught to our medical lore,
In nineteen-hundred and ninety-four.

In that year of our Lord——it seems wondrous to say——
We'll e'en generate babies in a new-fangled way!
No dreary, protracted obstetrical cases,
No frightened young doctors with terror-drawn faces;
No placenta-praevia, post-partum trouble,
No mal-presentations and infants born double——
For we'll hatch out our babes in an incubator,
In nineteen-hundred and ninety-four.

And the following sign we will hang on the wall,
To be read by each patient that happens to call;
"Fifty cents for a baby—the lowest price yet!
Make your choice, gentle folk—either blond or brunette.
Turn the knob to the right, if you're wanting a girl;
If a boy is your choice, give the left one a whirl,"
As for twins? Why we'll have 'em in colors galore,
In nineteen-hundred and ninety-four.

As we'll have a sure help for humanity's ills,
So we'll have a sure way of collecting our bills;
Some ready, exact, and infallible plan
That will make a rogue act out the part of a man.
And instead of complaining of liberal fees,
The rascals will drop on their tremulous knees
And will really feel hurt that we will not take more—
In nineteen-hundred and ninety-four.

We'll have things so arranged at that far future date,
That a man will not be the mere plaything of fate;
Compelled to go out in the rain and the cold,
To wait on the sick, the infirm, and the old,—
For, by means of a network of telephone wire,
We will study each case as we sit by the fire;
And by means of a pneumatic system at hand,
We'll distribute our medicines over the land.

But a word, worthy sires, and I hasten to close—
Let each take the path that's ahead of his nose;
Caring not for the narrow and tortuous track—
Full of ruts and obstructions—that lies at his back.
Let each do his best, and contribute his mite
Of a candle to banish the blackness of night;
And our praises will echo the wide world o'er,
In nineteen-hundred and ninety-four.

By S.Q. Lapius

· · · · · ·

Let's Do It

Let's wail and cry and refuse to buy—
    Let's grouch and refuse to sell;
Be it fair or fowl, let's growl and howl,
    And act as foolish as—well,
Just act as foolish and mad and mulish
    As any benighted Turk;
Then eject the spleen that makes us mean—
    And buckle down to work!

Let's decline to spend and refuse to lend
    And complain that the weather's hot;
And declare and swear that Fate's unfair—
    And the world has gone to pot.
Let's get off the job and join the mob
    Of loafers, and shift and shirt;
And then blush in shame at the silly game—
    And buckle down to work!

Let's fizz and fuss and discuss and cuss
    The Congress and the President;
And groan and sigh about taxes high,
    And bemoan about the rent.
Let's soak our souls in the slimy holes
    Of gloom, where the blue imps lurk;
And then come clean of our acrid spleen
    And all get down to work.

by J. B. Naylor

. . . . . .

Blowing Bubbles

Blowing bubbles – blowing bubbles—
　　'Tis the jolliest of sport!
Blowing bubbles clear and turbid,
　　Blowing bubbles long and short;
Puffed out cheeks and tangled tresses,
　　Dancing eyes and pursed up lips,
All in motion——all concentered
　　Where the dangling bubble drips!

Blowing bubbles——blowing bubbles—
　　Twain of merry maidens, they,
Blowing bubbles light and fragile,
　　Blowing bubbles bright and gay.
Quaint Lucile and roguish Olive—
　　Mark the dainty fingertips,
Gently toying with the pipe-stem
　　As the dangling bubble drips!

Blowing bubbles-blowing bubbles—
　　See, the puckered ruby lips
Blow a gale that snaps the moorings
　　Of this flimsiest of ships;
And across the airy billows
　　Does the fairy vessel sail
Till it lies a shapeless ruin
　　Wrecked upon a counter gale.

Blowing bubbles—blowing bubbles—
　　Ah! But grown-up children, we,
Blowing bubbles to our liking—
　　Blowing bubbles fair to see;
And the pearly, iridescent
　　Nothings cost a world of strife—
And their sum makes up the substance
　　Of the bubble we call life!

by S.Q. Lapius

. . . . . .

Laugh

Laugh — and the world laughs with you,
　　Weep — and it gives you the laugh;
Grin — and you'll get all the world owes
　　Grouch — and you won't get half.

by JBN

. . . . . .

The Fair

Comin' fair-time? My law-zee!
Let me whoop an' stretch my length—
Clear the track an' furnish me
Room accordin' to my strength.
'Tain't no use o'talkin' 'bout—
Blamed if I ain't fairly itchin'
Jest to fetch one lusty shout
'N' bust the belly-band 'r britchin'!
Funny how a feller feels
W'en the ginger's in his heels—
Cuttin' pigeon wings an' reels.
Same ol' season; same ol' air;
Same ol' feelin'; I declare,
That I ust to have—an' 'pears
Blowed aside an' left it bare—
Same ol' Morgan County Fair!

Don't I jest remember—Say?
How we ust to come fer miles,
Startin' at the peep o' day—
Wagon loads o' grub, an' piles
O' purty gals all smirks an' smiles;
Backwoods' manners, backwoods' styles—
Linsey-woolsey frocks an' gowns,
(Store clo'es was uncommon riches

Only wore by folks in towns,)
Cowhide boots an' linen britches!
Takin' in the shows an' races,
Munchin' peanuts, eatin' candy,
Huntin' out the shady places——
'N' makin' love w'en it come handy!
Blest if I don't feel today,
Like my pore ol' withered soul
Blossomed out as fresh an' gay
As a striped "barber pole."
Same ol' season, same ol' air——
Same ol' Morgan County Fair!

Am I goin'? Well, I guess!
Jim Rusk says she'll be a go——
'N' ever'body mus' confess
If it's in the Herald, it is so.
Ain't been there for sev'ral years,
Sence I proved myself an ass——
Bought some pewter runnin' gears
In as case o' polished brass
That the feller called a watch;
Claimed the cheap an' worthless botch
Solid gold, an' worked to catch
Pore ole silly fools like me.
Ain't been back there sense then, See!

But this long-laiged Jim Rusk, he
Says this fair'll be "OK—"
Somethin' like they ust to be;
Floral hall in grand array,
Lots o' stock an' big display
O' everything. An' look here—Say!
My ol' heart's keyed up in tune
Swellin' like a toy balloon;
Almos' bustin', I declare,
For an ol'-time county fair!

There's a goin' to be some shows
Worth the seein---Jim Rusk knows!
Trottin' matches, races, too;
P'fessor Wentz's 'quatic crew—
Wonder what that means, don't you?
Then a lot o' boys in tubs
Paddlin' cross the river wide,
Spinnin' round like wagon hubs
'Fore they reach the other side.
Allie Coulson's gone an' spent
Sever'l dollars—bought a tent
'N' trigged it out as grand as sin,
Jest to show his groundhog in!
Will Rusk's cross-eyed curious coon
Eatin' from a silver spoon,

An' Doc Naylor's parrot bird
Talkin' talk you never heard
'Ll ockypy a corner there—
At <u>this</u> Morgan County Fair.

Comin' fair-time? My, law-zee!
Let me whoop an' stretch my length—
Clear the track an' furnish me
Room accordin' to my strength.
Blest if I don't feel today,
Like my pore ol' withered soul
Blossomed out as fresh an' gay
As a striped "barber pole!"
My ol' heart's keyed up in tune,
Swellin' like a toy balloon
Boundin' up to reach the moon,
Same ol' season; same ol' air;
Same ol' feelin', I declare,
That I ust to have—an' 'pears
Like the mists o' thirty years
Rolled aside an' left it bare—
Same old Morgan County Fair!

by S.Q. Lapius (1985)

• • • • • •

Three Wise Monkeys

Three wise monkeys of Ancient Ind
Soberly sat — but slyly grinned.
The first no evil ever saw—
In monkey nature discovered no flaw;
The second no evil ever heard—
Never a syllable, sentence or word;
The third no evil ever spoke—
In deadly earnest or lively joke.
So they soberly sat, but slyly grinned—
The three wise monkeys of ancient Ind.

by J. B. Naylor

. . . . . .

Good Wishes

If good wishes were gold dollars,
    I'll tell you what I'd do:
I'd buy the boundless universe——
    And give it all to you!

And had I, too, the magic art
    And power——upon my soul!
I'd turn the blue sky upside-down
    And use it as a bowl;
And in it I would place the globe,

    This big, round earth of ours,
And rinse it well in sparkling dew
    And garnish it with flowers;
And then I'd lead you to the board,
    And seat you there to view it,
And say: "This is your Christmas fruit!
    Go to it, friend——go to it!"

by James Ball Naylor

. . . . . .

When Dey Talks Base Ball

Oh! dey talk it in de darkness,
An' dey talk it in de light,
Dey talk it in de mornin',
Ans' dey talk it late at night;
Dey talk it froo de summer,
An' dey talk it in de fall—
Kase dey nebber stops a talkin'
When deys talks base ball!

Chorus—
Talk aroun', talk aroun', talk aroun', I say;
Talky froo de night-time an' dey talky all de day,
Talky froo de summer an' dey talky in de fall—
Kase dey nebber stops a talkin' when dey talks base ball!

Oh! dey tells you dat Bert Adams
Am a dandy on first base,
An' dey say dat Charley Pennell,
As a pitcher, leads de race:
While insistin' dat "Cue" Carroll,
As a ketcher, beats 'em all—
Kase dey nebber stops a talkin'
When dey talks base ball!

Chorus—
* * *

Ef you wants to see a coacher,
W'y jest take a peep at "Mack"—
When Clyde Henery slugs de ball, sir,
W'y dey nebber gits it back!
Kase dem Clippers all am daisies.
An' dey conquers great and small—
Fer dey nebber gets defeated
When deys plays base ball!

Chorus—
* * *

Oh! dere's Spence dat plays de short-stop,
An' dere's Ramsey on third base—
Yes, an' Bain an' "Snik" Gillespie
Hustlin' all aroun' de place—;
Ef you hol' a han' like dat, sir,
W'y you'll nebber hab a call—
Kase de Clippers ain't no puddin'
When dey plays base ball!

Chorus—
* * *

by S.Q. Lapius

. . . . . .

Razzer Jim

I's a tough an' common nigger, an' my name is Razzer Jim;
An' I hasn't no religion, an' I specks my chance is slim
Of scrougin' into heaben—speshly sence I up an' lied
'Bout de fight at Santerago an' de way Jack Macy died.
W'at? You wants to hear de story? Well, dar ain't a heap to tell—
'Cept we wrasseled fo' Ol' Glory in de hottes' kin' of hell.
It was seben come eleben—an' de craps was loaded, too—
An' we done a sight ob shootin' fo' de ol' Red, White an' Blue!

But de story? Well, I'll tell you. Down in Georgy, years ago,
Me an' Jack was kids togedder—whar de watermillions grow.
I was jes a pickaninny—fat an ragged, full of fun;
He, a starchy little 'ristocrat—a rich man's only son.
But it didn't make no differ'nce 'bout de clo'es upon our backs,
We was frien's from start to finish—I's a gibbin' you de facks.
An' our daddies had been playmates—one de marster, one de slabe;
His is in de legistacher—mine's a sleepin' in de grabe.

Well, we growed up fas' as saplin's—tough an' limber-like an' slim;
I had heaps ob lub fo' Jacky, he had heaps ob lub fo Jim,
I was still a coon—a nigger—jes' a common ignor'nt fool;
Jacky wasn't ten pounds bigger—but he'd read in books at school,
An' could make de smartes' teacher come to time an' toe de scratch—
But he wa'nt no good kerplunkin' in de watermillion patch.
W'y I knowed whar eb'ry million in de county could be foun',
An each rooster's halleluyer fo' a dozen miles aroun'!

So we hunted, fished an' frolicked up an' down de big bayou,
All de suny days ob summer—in our long dugout canoe.
Jacky used to read to me from books, I used to sing to him;

An' de white trash called us "Macy's twins—dat on'ry Jack an' Jim!"
Say! I can't bear to talk erbout dem times—an' dats a fack;
It brings a lump up in my froat—but not de ol' day back—
An' makes me tink ob how we said goodby an' parted, w'en
We woke up one sad mornin' an' diskibbered we was men.

My folks hadn't no book knowledge—an' dey libed from han' to mouf.
His folks started him to college, so he lef' de Sunny Souf
An' went Norf; an I was lonesome—an' I couldn't work n'r play.
But jes' moped aroun' an' worried kaze dey'd sent my pard erway.
Den at las' I got so dat I t'ought at I'ld die;
So I packed my ragged duds an' tole my mammy a goodby.
An' I hoofe it norf—an' say! Good folks, de troof jes' beats de ban'—
But in less'n six mont's after dat I was a reg'lar army man.

Well, often t'ought ob Jacky—wondered w'at he was erbout,
But I didn't see de kid no mo 'till de Cuban war broke out.
Den one day at Santerago, I was standin' in de line
W'en an officer come ridin' pas', a lookin' spruce an' fine;
An' I clapped my peepers on 'im, and bellered, "Jacky! Jack!"
Say! I clean forgot my trainin'—deed an' double-dat's a fack!
But he rode on down de line an neber eben said a word;
An' I watched him turn de corner—an' I t'ought he hadn't heard.

Purty soon we all broke ranks; an' I jes' hustled after him,
Hollerin', "Jacky! Jacky Macy! Don't you reckernize ol' Jim?"
Den he reigned his prancin' nag in, an he drawed hisse'f up so,
An' he said, "I's Cap'n Macy, I am pleased to let you know!
Won't you stan' aside, good feller, you's a makin' mos' too free.
I don't soshiate wid niggers—all coons look erlike to me!
An' I can't imagine hardly—an' he curled his lip an' swore—
"W'at you blacks is doin' down here, dis is jes' a white man's war!"

Say! He broke my heart—but den I didn't mean to let him know.
So I drawed myse'f up dis way, an' I said re'l hard an' slow:
"I salute you, Cap'n Macy! I's de roughes' toughes' limb
In de bloomin' reg'lar army—an' dey calls me Razzer Jim!
'N' if it wasn't fo' yo' shoulder straps, I'd tap you on de beak
An' shut yo' eyes so tight de wouldn't open fo' a week!"
Den I turned aroun' an' walked erway, an' lef' him in de lurch;
An' he set a starin' at me, like de clock-face on a church.

De nex' mornin', bright an' early, we got in de hottes' fight
Dat de ol' Nick eber hear ob—an' we kept' it up till night;
An' dem Spaniards was a shellin' us, from up dar on de hill—
An' many a Yankee trooper swallowed down a Spanish pill.
W'y dem Mauser balls was flyin' thicker'n bumblebees in June;
An' de air was full ob smoke—you couldn't see de sun at noon,
Well, I stood dar loadin'—shootin', till de sweat dripped from my nose;
An' I t'ought I'd starve to deaf—I'd no tobaker in my clo'es!

All at once I seen a feller come a tearin' down de slope,
Bellerin' like a calf a chokin' an' a bawlin' fo' mo' rope.
An' I knowed him in a minute—but my God! I staggered back,
An' I t'ought I was a dreamin', was dat pale-faced coward Jack!
Was dat my ol' comrade Jacky, dat I'd played wid many a day,
Dat was leabin' his comman'—an skeered to deaf an runnin' erway?
An' he hurt me mo' dat minute—dat's de solem troof, I know,
Dan w'en he fused to reckergnize me in de camp de night befo'!

I jes' dropped my gun an' grabbed him by de arm an' whirled him 'roun'
But his shakey legs de wilted—an he sunk upon de groun'.
Den I stooped an' jerked him to his feet, an' took him by de han'
An hollered, "Jack, fo' God's sake, hurry back to yo' comman'!"
But his white lips only whispered, "Let me go, Jim—let me go!

I has got de skeer upon me—an' I cannot face de foe!
I don't keer fo' fame ner glory"—and he panted hard to bref—
"Dar's no one to tell de story—let me go—I's skeered to deaf!"

Den an awful t'ing it happened—but I specks 'twas fo' de bes'—
One ob dem dar Mauser bullets foun' a home in Jacky's breas'!
So I laid him on de grass dar. Den I jes' picked up my gun—
An' I fit on like a demon, till de battle it was won.
W'en dey foun' him in de ebenin', w'y de colonel sighed an' said,
"Dar's a bullet in his breas', boys; Cap'n Macy's wid de dead.
He was somew'at wild 'n' reckless, but his soul is safe, I know,
Fo' he died fo' flag an' country—an his face was to de foe!"

I was wounded in de battle; so I crossed de biller's foam,
An' I went to see my mammy an' Jack's ol' folks down home.
Well, 'twas den I seared by conscience pas' redemption; fo' I lied
An' tole his gray-haired parents how he led de charge an' died.
An' his weepin' mammy hel' my han' an' murmured sof' 'n' low;
"It's easy now to gib him up—his face was to de foe!"
Oh! I's jes a common nigger! An' I specks my chance is slim
Oh scroungin' into heaben, kase I's tough—I's Razzer Jim!

by S.Q. Lapius (1899)

· · · · · ·

Eloise

I.

Eloise, darling, be gracious to me,
All through the springtime I've waited for thee;
Waited and longed while the birds and the bees
Warbled and whispered of sweet Eloise.
Now that the summer is here and the skies
Rival the tint of thy beautiful eyes,
Leave me no longer to languish and pine—
Eloise, Eloise, darling, be mine!
    Cheeks like the roses and clover,
    Lips like the honey and wine,
    Eyes with true love brimming over—
    Eloise, darling, be mine!
    Leave me no longer to languish.
    Leave me no longer to pine,
    Pity me, love, in mine anguish—
    Eloise, darling, be mine!

II.

Eloise, darling, the autumn is here,
Leaves of the woodland are withered and sere;
Meadows are brown, and the golden rod fair
Rivals the gold of thy sunshiny hair.
List, thee, my darling, be gracious I pray,
Ere the bright autumn has faded away;
Leave me no longer to languish and pine—
Eloise, Eloise, darling, be mine!
    Teeth like the pearls—how they glisten!
    Eyes like the stars—how they shine!
    Ears like the sea shells—Ah listen:
    Eloise, darling, be mine!
    Leave me no longer to languish,
    Leave me no longer to pine,
    Pity me, love, in mine anguish—
    Eloise, darling, be mine!

III.

Eloise, darling, the autumn is past:
Winter is here, and the voice of the blast
Murmurs thy name as it moans through the trees,
Telling of love and sweet Eloise.
May the white snowflakes, that riding the storm
Rival the grace of thy beautiful form,
Bear thee this message—Oh! rapture divine—
Eloise, Eloise, darling be mine!
    Hair like the sunbeams at noonday,
    Lips like the honey and wine,
    Breath like the breath of a June day—
    Eloise, darling, be mine!
    Leave me no longer to languish,
    Leave me no longer to pine,
    Pity me, love, in mine anguish—
    Eloise, darline, be mine!

by S.Q. Lapius

. . . . . .

A Tailor-Made Suit

He fell on his knees and he earnestly prayed:
"Be kind, my heart PANTS to in-VEST in a maid:
I am DYEING of love—Oh! I cannot live SEW.—
If I get what I NEEDLE be happy I know.

He thus PRESSED his SUIT, but she said, "I declare
I'll never consent BUTTON route to the fair.
You must SLEEVE me forever, unless you can pay
The expenses, dear sir, for we can't SPONGE our way."

"I am WORSTED," he said, "and the battle is lost—
Why it makes my CHINCHILLA to think of the cost!
You're a silly young GOOSE, thus to trifle with men."
And he took up the THREAD of his travels again.

by James Ball Naylor

. . . . . .

Verse inscribed in a copy of <u>The Sign of the Prophet</u> sold for the benefit of the Red Cross War Fund, at McConnelsville, Ohio—April 20, 1918:

Who buys this little book of mine—
He does an act that's half divine;
Because the coin he pays shall be
Made consecrate to Liberty.
So blessings rest on him, I pray,
From this time forth—and night and day!

James Ball Naylor

. . . . . .

Sign on the Office Door:

We have but one office rule—one, and no more!
By which every caller is bound to abide:
Don't stop to knock when you come to the door—
Nor begin to knock when you get inside.

James Ball Naylor

. . . . . .

Two Men Of Our Town

There is a man in our town,
Who <u>thinks</u> he's wondrous wise,
And when he goes to drive a nail
He closes both his eyes.

And when he finds he's missed the nail,
He yells with might and main,
And shuts his eyes the closer and
He misses it again!

He pays two prices for a cheap,
Ill fitting suit — the J!
And grumbles at the price of clothes
Forever and for A!

There is a man in our town,
And he <u>is</u> wondrous wise,
Who hits the nail upon the head
'Most every time he tries.

He goes to Walker's clothing store—
The "Old Standby's", you know—
And buys a rich and stylish suit,
And buys it wondrous low.

And when he comes to try it on,
It fits him to a T;
And so he smiles at Arch and sings:
You've saved me just a V!

by S.Q. Lapius

(The above was written as a bit of advertising.)

Billy Bryan

Oh, the sun shall shine forever,
    And the world with music ring,
And the winter days shall never
    Hush the bluebird's song of spring
When we've won the fight for silver
    By a ballot battle fair,
And have seated Billy Bryan
    In the White House chair.

For the money kings shall grumble
    At the Yankee eagle's scream,
And the factory spindle's rumble
    To the hiss of rushing steam,
And the British lion cower
    In his black and bloody lair—
When we've seated Billy Bryan
    In the White House chair.

All the land shall glow with gladness
    From the mountains to the sea,
And there'll be no place for sadness
    When the Workingman is free,
And the shining road to heaven
    Shall be up the silver stair—
When we've seated Billy Bryan
    In the Whie House chair.

Ah, the shaggy wolf of hunger
    Shall be driven from the land
When the good old "daddy dollar"
    Is in the grimy toiler's hand;
And the earth shall groan with plenty
    And the poor man have his share—
When we've seated Billy Bryan
    In the White House chair.

by S.Q. Lapius

· · · · · ·

The Whole Year Round

Oh! there ain't no use a grievin'
Pretendin' or believin'
That all the year is dark an' drear
With bleak an' barren ground;
That the winter days dissever
The summer days forever.
    An' It's night time—
    An' fright time
The whole year round!

For the peep o' day is comin',
The busy bees 're hummin'——
The'r backs an' wings, an' legs an' stings
With honey gaumed an' drowned;
An' the sunlight siftin' over
The fields o' dewy clover
    Tell it's daytime—
    An' May Time—
The whole year round!

So there ain't no use contendin'
That night is never endin'——
That winter's here, an' all the year
The earth is stripped and browned;
For the sun an' shade a-shiftin',
An' the apple blooms a driftin'
    Tell it's noon time—
    An June time—
The whole year round!

by S.Q. Lapius

The Rabbit's Tale

Said the fox to the rabbit: "I hear
    You know a rare tale of good cheer.
    If you'd hear me your friend,
    With a view to that end,
Come whisper your tale in my ear."

Quoth the rabbit, "It isn't my forte
    To tell stories and things of that sort.
    I know but one tail"—
    And he fled like a gale—
"And that one's exceedingly short!"

by J. B. Naylor

. . . . . .

To The High And Mighty County Commissioners

You are building a bridge for the county—
     And it's costing enough, heaven knows!
Have respect for our liberal bounty,
     And leave us a dime in our clothes!
But while you are spanning the river—
     And cementing the piers with our "glue,"
Must we stand on the margin and shiver—
     And swear at the "Katy" and you?

We've appealed for an adequate ferry;
     Your thumbs in your vest-holes you jammed,
Elevated your chins with a —"Nary!"
     And said: "Let the public be damned!
We are priests of the censer and psalter—
     Ye are mendicants out at the knees;
We've the taxpayers neck in the halter—
     And we'll spend his hard cash as we please."

We have brought to your august attention,
     That the voyage from town unto town
Is a wearisome one; at the mention
     You remarked: "Go way back and sit down!"
We have plead that our lives are in danger,
     That we have no desire to be wrecked;
You replied: "You're a beggar, a stranger,
     With no rights we are bound to respect!"

Good sirs, we are humble and lowly—
    And meekly we'll take what ye give;
Oh, Commissioners mighty and holy,
    Still grant us permission to live!
For, oh, if the ferry o'er "Jordan"
    Is as bad as the one you provide,
We prefer to bear life and its burden—
    And forever remain on this side!

       by S.Q. Lapius

. . . . . .

The Big Wood Fire

Away with yer gas an' yer furnace heat,
    Yet bituminous coal an' yer anthracite!
Give me the priv'lege of shovin' my feet
    Under the ol'-fashioned dog-irons bright,
Let me loll back in my splint-bottom chair—
    Happy's the mortal whose warmest desire
Is toastin' his shins by the flicker an' flare,
    That comes from the depths of the big wood fire!

Spite o' time's changes, the ol' fireplace looks
    Jest like it did in the days o' my youth,
When I bent low over papers an' books—
    Siftin' the chaff for a few grains o' truth.
Up on the mantle the ol' wooden clock—
    Feelin' the spell o' the time an' the place—
Numbers the hours with a merry tick-tock
    An a shadowy smile on its sunny ol' face.

Pap doin' over his paper an' pipe—
    Feet on the jamb an' his nose toward the skies—
Grumbles a little, a-thinkin' the type
    Somewhat too dim for his sleepy ol' eyes;
Mam drops 'er knittin'—fer Mam likes a joke—
    An' nudgin' my ribs as a vigorous hint,
Whispers, "Yer pap's got his eyes full o' smoke—
    Hear him a-scoldin' the editor's print!"

Lazy ol' farm dog asleep on the floor,
      Head on his paws an' a-dreamin' o' game;
Big tabby cat by the settin'-room door,
      Dozin' an' purrin' an' doin' the same.
Pap drops his paper an' drops off to sleep,
      Mam winds her knittin', I put up my slate;
Ol' wooden clock 'round the room takes a peep
      An' ticks off the words, "Gittin' late—gittin' late!"

Big room deserted an' everything still,
      Fire burnin' low an' the blaze dyin' out;
Snow pilin' high on the wide winders sill,
      Long, lanky shadders a-creepin' about;
Ol' timepiece a-talkin' away to itself—
      Mumblin' a kind of a sleepy tick-tock—
Stands there alone on the high mantle shelf.
      Everyone sleepin' but God an' the clock!

Then away with yer fires made o' gas an' coal;
      They give me the shivers—they do, I swan!
They burn up the body, but freeze out the soul—
      Give me the fire of the days long gone.
Grant me the priv'lege o' shooin' my feet
      Under the ol'-fashioned dog-irons bright,
Little I'll reck o' the snow er sleet
      Er the howl o' the wind on a winter night!

by S. Q. Lapius

. . . . . .

Bit of Verse

(after election day 1910)

Then here's to the dear departed
Who fell in the recent strife;
Brothers of mine, brave-hearted—
Each fought to preserve his life.
So, ghosts of the game, stand steady,
Let's swap a few quips and jokes;
Here's a cheer for the killed already—
And hurrah for the next that croaks.

Old Clarkie's spirit is harking
Away over hill and vale—
And his hounds are loudly barking
Far off on a lonesome trail.
But, the rest of you, all stand steady—
Some fellow pass around the smokes,
Here's a glass to the dead already—
And hurrah for the next that croaks.

John McBee and Lester Williams,
Brace up here and toe the crack;
Your elusive five-dollar billiams
Are gone—and they won't come back.
So stand in your places steady—
Be careful that no man chokes;
Let's drink to the dead already
And hurrah for the next that croaks.

George Hughes and Carlos Thompson,
Jim Johnson and Jim Monroe—
And every man who had comps on
His own individual show.
Line up in your places steady;
Let's win the applause of folks.
Now!—a glass to the dead already
And hurrah for the next that croaks!

by James Ball Naylor

. . . . . .

The Old-Time Friend

The old-time scenes of old-time days—a
The old-time joys and games and plays!
Ah, how their memories merge and blend
In one dear thought—
    The old-time Friend!

When years were young and life was new,
The old-time friend was good and true;
And so we say today: Fate lend
To each and all—
    An old-time Friend.

The old-time Friend! Whose word and smile
Oft cheered us onward, mile on mile;
Who, when we fell, would kindly bend
And lift us up—
    The old-time Friend.

Ah, Spring may pass and summer go,
And autumn come, and winter show,
But life is love, and so I send
These lines to you—
    An old-time Friend!

by James Ball Naylor

Published as booklet by Rust Craft in 1912

Across the Miles

True friendship! With the thought appears
    Your jolly face, your happy smiles.
We may not meet for days or years,
    But let's shake hands across the miles.

Aye, let's shake hands across the miles,
    The miles of sea, the miles of shore,
And trust the kindly afterwhiles
    May bring us face to face once more.

Though one may gaze on fields of snow,
    The other look on fields of green,
We're old-time comrades still, I know
    No matter are the miles between.

The fates have lured us far apart,
    I miss you, and I miss your smiles;
But friendship holds us, heart to heart,
    So let's shake hands across the miles.

by James Ball Naylor

Published as booklet by Rust Craft in 1912

For You

If I could have my will and way,
And hour by hour, and night and day,
The changing seasons through;
I'd make the whole year bright and fair,
And free from sorrow, want and care;
And do it all for YOU.

By day I'd have the sun to guide
Your footsteps, that no ill betide,
Nor danger meet your view—
To light the path would lead you toward
Your duty and its full reward;
All this I'd do for YOU.

By night I'd have the moon above
To serve you as a lamp of love,
To help you to hold true
The course whereon your feet should press,
In dreams, the glades of happiness;
And all for you—for YOU.

And more, I'd have Good Fortune stand,
With smiling face and outstretched hand,
To bless and lead you to
The richest stores of worldly wealth—
The goodly land of perfect health;
I'd do it all—for YOU.

by James Ball Naylor

(Published as a booklet by Rust Craft in 1912)

· · · · · ·

If You Were Here

If you were here, the clouds of gray
In golden mist would melt away;
The sun shine bright, the skies prove clear,
And all be well, if you were here.

The birds would sing a gleesome song
To welcome you the whole day long;
The bees would herald far and near
The cheering news, if you were here.

And I would think my every care,
My every burden, light as air;
Forget that life was ever drear,
And just be glad, if you were here.

If you were here, if I could see
Your smiling face today, ah—me!
This world would be a place of cheer
And happiness, if you were here.

by James Ball Naylor

(Published as a booklet by Rust Craft in 1912)

On With The Dance!

A penny saved is a penny earned!
Well, save your pence—I'm not concerned:
The highway that invites my soul,
Where every vagabond may stroll,
Accepts a merry song as toll!

Let others toil and moil; I'll dance
In care-free joy—and take my chance!
Yes, let him work who will or must;
Some kindly soul, I hope and trust,
Will furnish me my daily crust.

by J. B. Naylor

· · · · · ·

After the Day—The Dark

September 9, 1916

After the day—the dark, dear!
The morning of life was fair;
    And the moon was bright
    With radiant light—
And the evening free from care.
    But after the fall
    Of dusk comes the call
For a further journey—hark!
After the day—the dark, dear!
    After the day—the dark!

After the day—the dark, dear!
The day has been smooth—and rough;
    The skies have been blue
    And friends have been true—
And life has been good enough.
    But the shadows fall
    And envelope all—
And is there a guiding spark?
After the day—the dark, dear!
    After the day—the dark!

After the day—the dark, dear!
And will there be, at the end
 Of the road, a light
 To guide us aright—
A light in the house of a friend?
 Will a kindly hail
 Be borne on the gale—
Out of the blackness stark?
After the day—the dark, dear!
 After the day—the dark!

After the day—the dark, dear!
And where will the journey cease—
 In the darkness vast,
 Or shall we at last
Reach a golden land—and peace?
 Does the road, perforce
 Stretch an endless course—
And with never a sign nor mark?
After the day—the dark, dear!
 After the day—the dark!

by James Ball Naylor

. . . . . .

Brown October

(1918)

Brown October, take my hand!
As explorers brown and bold,
Eager to possess the land—
All its wealth to have and hold;
As marauders of the field,
Pillagers of orchard fruit,
Robbers of the woodland's yield,
Gatherers of luscious loot,
Let's be off——to ramble on,
Just as in the years agone!

Brown October, come with me!——
Far across the pasture lands
Where the old persimmon tree,
In its gnarled and withered hands,
Clutches close its precious crop—
Yet, at every breeze's nod,
Loosens up its grip to drop
Countless jewels on the sod.
Let's be off——to romp and climb,
Just as in the olden time!

Brown October, here we go!
Merrymen of glen and glade,
Fellows with the winds that blow,
Cronies with the sheen and shade;
Ours the pawpaw's gleaming gold,
Ours the autumn's heady wine,
Ours the gems and wealth untold
Of the nut tree and the vine.
Let's be off; the woodland ways
Lure us, as in olden days!

Brown October, tarry—wait!
Glance aback, and lo! You'll see
I'm a little more sedate—
Older than I used to be;
In my eyes you'll note the haze
Of the crisping autumn air,
And the frost of autumn days
Powdering my scanty hair.
Let's be off; but let your speed
Measure with your comrade's need!

by James Ball Naylor

. . . . . .

What's the Use?

A daily fight, a war of years!
And wounds, and scars, and toil and tears—
Bald scheme and ruse!
To earn a place, to gain a name—
A foretaste of tomorrow's fame!
Ah, what's the use!

A dusty book of verse or plays,
A grinning skull—the world's mad praise,
Or vain abuse!
A withered bit of faded bay—
Forgotten fame of yesterday!
And what's the use!

by J.B.N.

Naylor's Bookplate
Courtesy of Robert Naylor.

War

Hell's a-poppin';
Bombs 're droppin',
From the skies——and
Hates's out-cropping'.
This is war.

Airplanes zoomin',
Big guns boomin';
Every patriot
Now finds room in
Such mad war!

In past ages
Holy sages
Prayed for peace——but
Hist'ry's pages
Tell of war.

Present tenses
Stir our senses;
We must build up
Our defenses——
Gird for war!

Earth's o'er crowded,
Thinking's clouded,
Reason's dead and
Wisdom's shrouded.
War——oh, war!

by James Ball Naylor

The Call and The Answer

Old England called to her stalwart sons—
    To her sons across the seas,
And she said, "The blows of my ruthless foes
    Have brought me to my knees:
As you needed me in your infancy—
    I need you now in my age.
You're young; you're free—will you stand by me,
    In a battle I must wage?"

And they answered her—those loyal sons:
    "Though a thousand leagues divide,
And the way be set with grave dangers, yet
    You will find us at your side.
We are one in heart, we are one in hand,
    We are one in purpose true;
And blood is thicker than water, and—
    Old Mother, we'll stand by you."

And they went—those sons, those loyal ones,
    To the Mother over the seas:
From the Arctic lands and the tropic sands
    And the far Antipodes.
And with bated breath, they diced with death,
    And gave all they had to give—
Gave home and health and life itself,
    That the Mother-land might live.

Oh, you stalwart sons, you loyal ones,
　　May you not give up the fight;
May your feet be shod with the wrath of God,
　　Till you conquer for the right.
For you war for peace—that war may cease,
　　And peace may have new birth;
That love and light and freedom bright,
　　May reign o'er all the earth.

by James Ball Naylor

"Verses written by James Ball Naylor, of Malta, Ohio, U.S.A., on learning of the death of a young Australian, William Charles Hicks, of Melborne, one of the great army of Australian's heroes slain in the war against the Beast of Berlin."

· · · · · ·

Hands Across The Sea Again

It's hands across the sea again—
　　It's hands across the sea!
For English-speaking peoples swear
　　They'll stay forever free.
America is mad as hell,
　　And Britain's heart is full,
So Uncle Sam puts forth his hand
　　And Shakes with Johnny Bull.

It's hands across the sea again—
　　It's hands across the sea!
The lusty Hun is making war,
　　The Jap is on a spree;
But we'll stand straight to meet our fate—
　　And we'll not care a damn!—
For Johnny Bull puts forth his hand
　　And shakes with Uncle Sam.

It's hands across the sea again—
　　It's hands across the sea!
And we have formed a union strong—
　　The great A-B-C-D;
And every member grabs the line
　　And gives a mighty pull,
Since Uncle Sam puts forth his hand—
　　And shakes with Johnny Bull.

It's hands across the sea again—
  It's hands across the sea!
For freedom-loving folks won't stand
  The chains of slavery.
The Russians knock the Nazis—
  They rout 'em in a jam,
When Johnny Bull puts forth his hand,
  And shakes with Uncle Sam.

by James Ball Naylor

. . . . . .

The Real Truth

An eye for an eye,
A tooth for a tooth!
Let's not tell a lie—
Let's tell the bare truth.
Of course we'll show mercy—
Where mercy is shown;
But we'll never show mercy
Where mercy's unknown.

It's war to the knife
And knife to the hilt—
Where their blood-stained blades
Show their fiendish guilt.
It's no time for tolerance,
No time for tears;
We'll fight as we fought
Through the multiple years.

"Remember Pearl Harbor!"
"Remember the Maine!"
"Remember the Alamo!"
Every man slain.
Remember the Big Horn,
Where brave Custer died—
His sword in his hand,
His steed at his side!
We'll fight on the land,

We'll fight on the sea,
We'll fight in the air;
And we'll remain free!
Yea, vengeance is ours!
We'll master our might
And show foreign serfs
How free Yankees can fight!

by James Ball Naylor

· · · · · ·

YOU

The laddie in uniform marches away
Marches under the Red, White, and Blue;
He goes forth to enter the murderous fray—
And, remember, he does it for you!
He sweeps o'er the sea, or he swoops through the air,
Or camps on the battle-front grim;
He's doing and daring for you over there!
Say! What are You doing for him?

He eats in a shack, or a dugout so deep
It's as damp and as dark as a well;
He dreams of a heaven of home in his sleep—
But he lives in perpetual hell!
He fights day and night, when the midday is fair,
When the midnight is ghostly and dim;
He's daring and doing for You over there!
Say! What are You doing for Him?

He serves in the clouds, and he slaves in the mud—
And holds himself steadfast and true;
He gives of his brain and his brawn and his blood—
And does it, remember, for You!
Every day he dares death, every hour braves a snare—
Puts in pawn every member and limb;
He's doing and Dying for you over there!
Say! What are You doing for Him?

by James Ball Naylor

After-Thought

Yes, I've heard that voice in the lonesome night—
    That call of the restless sea;
And I heard it sing like a living thing—
    And it brought this message to me:

"The world's at war, on my farther shore;
    And the weeds of hate, long grown,
Have ripened at last in a harvest vast—
    And their seeds o'er my waves have blown.

"And they foul the water, and fill the air—
    And blot out the sun of the right;
There is day no more, from shore to shore—
    But only the hell of night.

"And murderous deeds, by maddened men,
    Are done in the name of war;
And great ships go down, and their people drown—
    And deep darkness hovers o'er."

Yes, I've heard that call in the lonesome night—
    That song in a minor key:
A sad lullaby to the souls that lie
    Asleep in the bed of the sea!

by James Ball Naylor

I've Missed So Much
(1922)

I've travelled with the winding way of life,
Where with blessings the fields and woods are rife;
Yet today the burden of my song
Is: I've missed so much as I passed along!

I've seen the beauties of rill and vale,
I've heard the bird songs of hill and dale;
I've enjoyed the solitude, loved the throng—
But I've missed so much as I passed along!

I've fraternized with comrade and friend—
And I've known a love that knows no end;
I've learned the right, and I've done the wrong—
Still, I've missed so much as I passed along!

I've done my worst, and I've done my best—
And kept the counsel within my breast;
And today I'm happy, hale and strong—
Yet, I've missed so much as I passed along!

by James Ball Naylor

. . . . . .

Her Answer
(1922)

Yes, you've missed a lot as you passed along,
Yet you've known the notes of the wild bird's song.
You have drunk in the sunshine;
You've loved Nature's flowers;
You've seen winter's snows;
And you've seen summer's showers.
The gnarled old oak, with its arms outspread,
Has oft been a canopy over your head.
Yes, all of these things, and more I say,
Have not been missed as they passed your way.

Life is a circus of so many rings,
One can't help missing a lot of good things.

by Lucile Naylor

. . . . . .

The Nicest Tree Of All

The chestnut-tree is a dear old tree,
  With its leaves so glossy-green,
And the maple-tree makes the coolest shade
  That ever I have seen.
The hickory-tree is a fine old tree—
  So straight and clean and tall;
But of all the trees the Christmas-tree
  Is the nicest tree of all.

The apple-tree is a useful tree,
  And the cherry and peach are, too;
If we had no fruit to eat, I guess
  We wouldn't know what to do.
How I like the blossoms in the spring
  And the apples in the fall—
But of all the trees, the Christmas-tree
  Is the nicest tree of all.

The plum-tree bears the sweetest blooms
  Of any tree, in spring.
And the pawpaw-tree bears the latest fruit—
  And as good as anything!
The beech-tree gives its creamy nuts,
  And the sycamore-tree, its balls;
But of all the fruit, the Christmas-tree
  Bears the nicest fruit of all.

by James Ball Naylor

. . . . . .

Who Deserves The Honor

The Rubaiyat! The Rubaiyat!
Who was it swung the mighty bat
That knocked a swift and lofty homer—
Was it Fitzgerald or old Omar?

The Rubaiyat! The Rubaiyat!
To both great men I lift my hat.
'Twas in old Omar's brain that swirled
The thoughts Fitzgerald gave the world.

The Rubaiyat! The Rubaiyat!
We prate of this—we prate of that.
Khayyam—an ancient, unknown sage;
Fitzgerald brought him to our age.

by James Ball Naylor

· · · · · ·

The Pioneer of the Air
(Written in 1927 at the time of Lindbergh's flight)

I'm the buoyant, agile and free
Final craft of the Powers that Be;
    And I swoop and I swerve,
    And I circle and curve—
I'm the ship of the Uppermost Sea.
With my white sails outspread, and my prow
Pointing high o'er the luminous brow
    Of the cloud mountains, I
    Cleave my way through the sky;
I'm the marvel of Nineteen-and-now.

Wings—to keep time to the breeze as it sings
    Songs of adventure and quest:
Tail—to disport with the tempest or gale—
    Ho, for the East and the West!

I'm the sum of the deeds Man has done,
I'm the substance of victories won;
    The vague dream of the vast
    Many centuries past—
And the fact of the one now begun.
And the sunshiny air-billows, whirled
Right and left by my swift keel and curled
    Into vaporous spray,
    One by one fall away
O'er the farthermost rim of the world.

Wings—to give hail to the breeze as it brings
    Word of wet weather or drought:
Tail—to wigwag to the tempest or gale—
    Ho, for the North and the South!

I'm the scion of races outworn,
I'm the sire of great peoples unborn;
    And my scintillant wake
    Is the path Man must take—
As he travels from midnight to morn.
For my white sails outspread, and my prow
Pointing high o'er the luminous brow
    Of the cloud mountains steep,
    Find a way through the deep;
I'm the marvel of Nineteen-and-now.

Wings—to give heed to the breeze as it brings
    Promise of worst or of best:
Tail—to take care of the tempest or gale—
    Ho, for the East and the West!

by James Ball Naylor

· · · · · ·

From the Kansas City Star
(1929-1933)

Monday—we'll say is our "Heatless Day":
    One cinder, one flicker, one coal.
Tuesday—well this is our "Meatless Day";
    One oyster, one herring, one sole.
Wednesday—Oh, this is our "Wheatless Day";
    One corn cake, one dodger, one scone.
Thursday—we must have a "Sweetless Day";
    One pickle, one lemon, one bone.
Friday—will make a good "Eatless Day";
    One cheerful and glorious fast.
Saturday—call it a "Treatless Day,"
    For all reciprocities past.
But Sunday—may Hoover forgive us, we pray,
    If we should happen to feel
A little more hungry than usual today—
    And once again eat a square meal.

by Author Unknown

James Ball Naylor's Reply

Though Monday, good friend, may be "Heatless Day,"
    There's no need of getting cold feet;
Though Tuesday, indeed, may be "Meatless Day,"
    Your bones are still covered with meat.
Though Wednesday's the day you call "Wheatless Day,"
    Don't loaf at the table and glower;
And Thursday, old boy, may be "Sweetless Day,"
    Don't let your temper go sour.
And Friday, remember, is "Eatless Day"—
    So keep your mouth shut and don't bite;
And Saturday—well, if it's "Treatless Day,"
    Just use it to treat people right.
As for Sunday, you don't work on Sunday, you know—
    There, there, now—don't draw a long face—
You don't need much food, as it's easy to show,
    So use Sunday for fasting and grace!

· · · · · ·

Bully Yankee

(With apologies to Rudyard Kipling—but none to Herbert Hoover.)

We took a trip to Washington, to ask for bonus pay;
The President he ups an' says: "You'd better go away!
The railroads an' big bankers 're a-waitin' at the gate,
To lug away our money-bags—you'd better hop a freight!"
Oh, it's Bully this, an' Bully that, an'—"Bully you've got fleas!"
But its: "Grab y'r gun an' face it!—when there's hell across the seas.
When there's hell across the seas, old pards—there's hell across the seas;
It's—"Grab y'r gun an' face it!"—when there's hell across the seas!

We made our trip to Washington, to get some promised pay;
The Senate laughs, an' says: "Git out—no cash fer you today!
You're costin' too much money; an' us Mucky-Mucks o' state
'Ave come to the c'nclusion that we guess you'll 'ave to wait."
Fer it's Bully this, an' Bully that, an—"Bully, scoot pell-mell!"
But it's: "Bully, you're a hero!"—when we're fightin' in hot hell;
A-fightin' in hot hell, old pards, a-fightin' in hot hell.
Yes—"Bully, you're a hero!"—when we're fighting in hot hell!

Oh! makin' mock o' service Men, that kept you from all hurt,
Is cheaper than the pay they got—an' that was cheap as dirt!!
They've guarded us, an' worried us, an' clamped an' held us down;

Now Hoover's called the Reg'lars out—to prod us out o' town.
It's Bully this, an' Bully that, an' "Bully, what's the row?"
They used to have good use fer us—but ain't got any now!
We packed our kits, an' done our bits—an' let 'em have their say;
But—"Bully, you're a beggar!"—if you dare to ask fer pay!

We ain't no bloomin' heroes, n'r we ain't no scury jokes;
We're jest hard-luck Americans, in want—like other folks.
We tell 'em that we're hungry, an' we'd lie to keep alive;
They answer: "Jest wait patiently till nineteen forty-five!"
An' its Bully this, an Bully that, an'—Bully's name is mud!"
But Bully was a darlin'—when he shed his Yankee blood!
Yes, Bully was fit comp'ny then, fer ladies an' fer gents;
But now he is a dirty dog—when he asks for recompense!

We'll go back home and rest among the trees an' birds an' flowers;
An' wonder—yes, an' wonder!—if this country still is ours!
They've hurt us—hurt us deeper!—than the wounds that make us lame;
Our uniforms won't mean as much—the Flag won't seem the same!
Oh! it's Bully this, an' Bully that, an'—"Get to hell an' strive!
We won't have nothin' fer you—till you're dead, in Forty-Five."
Yes, dead in Forty Five, old pards—starved dead by Forty-Five!
They won't have nothin' fer us—till we're dead in Forty-Five!

by James Ball Naylor

The Elephant and The Tiger

An elephant and a tiger met
  Within a jungle cool;
The tiger saw his own neat dress
  Reflected in a pool;
And, being vain and frivolous,
  Remarked with caustic wit:
"My dear old fashioned rube, your clothes
  Are sadly out of style.
Your trousers bag about the knees,
  Your coat is quite too loose,
    Such lack of style
    Is simply vile—
And merits no excuse."

The Elephant, good naturedly, replied:
  "My city dude,
I must admit my garments are
  Old fashioned, quite, and rude;
But still I would not swap with you,
  Though you should offer boot;
I do not care to own or wear
  A striped prison suit.
However, you had better leave;
  I might, in sudden spunk—
    Denude your back
    And deftly pack
Your clothing in my truck!"

by James Ball Naylor

. . . . . .

The Baptismal Name of England's New King

Edward Albert Christian George
　　Andrew Patrick David:
On the lofty crag of fame,
　　Let that name be grave-ed.
Careful with your chisel, Fate
　　Let it all be sav-ed.
Edward Albert Christian George
　　Andrew Patrick David.

As a prince, full many a maid
　　And dame he met and brav-ed:
Edward Albert Christian George
　　Andrew Patrick David.
Now, as Britain's king, may he
　　Never prove deprav-ed:
Edward Albert Christian George
　　Andrew Patrick David.

Edward Albert Christian George
　　Andrew Patrick David:
May the bugles blare for him—
　　May the flags be brav-ed.
May the Empire find in him
　　All that it has craved:
Edward Albert Christian George
　　Andrew Patrick David.

by James Ball Naylor

. . . . . .

Then and Now

In years agone when this town was
  As wet as Noah's flood
When ardent liquor filled our veins;
  Instead of sluggish blood,
'Twas then, to keep our spirits up,
  We put the spirits down;
And ev'rybody called our burg—
    "The Old Rye Town."

It was so moist, in many homes,
  Folks couldn't raise a dust;
Society was soggy—all
  Except the upper crust;
And it was just a little damp,—
  There, there, you needn't frown!—
And drought was never dreamed of in—
    "The Old Rye Town."

But now things are so arid
  And so dry is ev'ry throat,
We find it hard to swallow down
  The local option vote;
Our crop of rye is blasted and
  Our hop vines have turned brown
And so we've changed our nickname to—
    "The Ol' Dry Town."

It's water, water ev'rywhere—
        But not a drop to drink,
Unless the soda-fountain man
        Will recognize our wink;
And water is so dangerous—
        In it some people drown.
Lord, love us and preserve us in
        "This Ol' Dry Town."

by James Ball Naylor

. . . . . .

The Old Liars' Bench

You may talk of the "church in the wildwood"
        Of the creek and the old "swimmin' hole,"
Of the glorified days of your childhood—
        Of your joys and your solace of soul;
But when age and its ailments assail you,
        Then the one place of sunshine and shade—
Where your ribs get a wrench—is the old "Liars' Bench"
        On the Courthouse colonnade.

You may boast of far-famed Marco Polo
        And the wandering life that he led;
You may brag of old Baron Munchausen—
        Still remember, they're both of 'em dead!
But of all present-day living liars
        Whose honors and laurels won't fade,
Their fingers still clench the old "Liars' Bench"
        On the courthouse colonnade.

They are there in the dew-dampened morning
        They are there in the mid-afternoon—
All their musty old tales re-adorning,
        All their tell-tattle tongues all atune;
But observe 'em sit pious and silent,
        Should it happen that matron or maid,
Or widow or wench, nears the old "Liars' Bench"
        On the courthouse colonnade.

by J. B. Naylor

Some Things You Can't Buy

Though you've plenty of money,
    And though you may try,
Here's a short list of things
    That you can never buy!

A sheet for the bed of the ocean,
    A safe for the bank of the brook,
A sock for the foot of a mountain—
    Watermelons as good as they look.

False teeth for the mouth of a cannon,
    A wig for the head of a drum,
Fresh meat for the hounds of a wagon—
    Five minutes of sweet Kingdom Come.

A fence for the yard of bleached muslin,
    Kid gloves for the hands of a clock.
Baled hay that will fatten a clothes horse—
    A Yankee insured not to knock.

A tin can for the tail of a comet,
    A sample of unalloyed bliss,
Enough water to fill the Big Dipper—
    A worse piece of nonsense than this.

by J. B. Naylor

The Shape of a Kiss

"What shape is a kiss?" asks a writer in a daily paper.

What shape's a kiss?
Well, I'll be bound,
One always likes
To have them round.
But lovers often
Lift a prayer
That kisses all
Be on the square.

And poets sing
This blightesome song:
"I have enjoyed
Your kisses long!"
What shape's a kiss?
The sweetest sort
I've always found—
Are far too short.

by J. B. Naylor

. . . . . .

Cold Weather Makes Us Anarchistic

When the weather drops to zero,
        We don't want to be a hero,
We just want to be old Nero—
        And set the town afire;
And without a grain of pity
        Sit and watch the burning city,
Play our fiddle, sing a ditty,
        And chortle and perspire!

by James Ball Naylor

· · · · · ·

The Prime Essential

What's the one thing—to be, to have, or to do—
necessary to success:

> Grit—says the grindstone;
> Push—remarks the wheelbarrow;
> Snap—asserts the ginger-cake;
> Going up—avers the aeroplane;
> Do your turn—ventures the earth;
> Stick to it—declares the glue;
> Hit the center—grins the target;
> Be keen—smiles the razor;
> Keep cool—chatters the ice;
> Stand firm—vows the mountain;
> Plug—murmurs the solder;
> Have an aim—says the gun.

by James Ball Naylor

. . . . . .

Birthday Greetings

You're thirty-two—and just a boy!
Why, think of all the love and joy,
And work and fellowship, in store
For you—for fifty years or more!
The man who keeps his heart in key
With duty, kindness, charity.
And tramps the many, many miles
Of mundane life, and smiles and smiles—
No matter if his hair turns gray.
No matter what the years may say—
Will always find himself among
The joys of life—and still be young!"

by James Ball Naylor

. . . . . .

The Old Chestnut Tree

Such an honest old tree!
And he smiled as he stood
Like a giant of eld,
In the edge of the wood;
For the summer was ended,
The autumn grown old—
And his pockets were bulging
With treasures of gold.

But that imp of the universe,
Cunning Jack Frost—
Caring much for a frolic
And naught for the cost!—
Won the old Chestnut's heart,
With his flattering wiles;
And the tree showered gold
In great glittering piles.

Not content with all this,
Jack must do even worse:
He induced the old fellow
To empty his purse.

Then he called in the Wind—
'Twas a little too bad!—
And together they took
All the old Chestnut had.

Yes, they left the old Chestnut
To hunger and cold,
And remorsely squandered
His treasures of gold;
And they chuckled and whistled
In infinite glee,
At the trick they had played
On the honest old tree!

by J. B. Naylor

· · · · · ·

Retribution

An angleworm was crawling forth to view the morning fair,
A sparrow spied the lowly worm—and ate it then and there;
But hardly had the sparrow gulped the wriggling morsel down—
When the bird was in the stomach of a weasel sleek and brown;
And barely had the weasel time to make a meal and run,
When a hawk swooped down upon it—and the weasel's life was done.

And thus it went: A prowling wolf, obeying hunger's call,
Pounced nimbly on the sated hawk—and ate it, bones and all;
And scarcely had the wolf had time to eat, and lick its paw,
Ere it was dead—and buried in a famished lion's maw;
Then the lion turned to slink away, but a rifle bullet sped—
And all at once the king of beasts was numbered with the dead.
That night the human hunter, kneeling on the lion's skin,
Besought the God of one and all to cleanse him from all sin;
And ended his petition thus: "Oh, Lord! With heart and mind
I thank thee that they righteous laws are merciful and kind!"

Of course, to carry out and finish up the scheme and plan
Of retribution, it's arranged that the Devil take the man:
But one thing I can't understand—my wits may be too slow—
Is: Who's to kill the Devil?
        That's the thing I want to know.

by James Ball Naylor

. . . . . .

Real Americanism

One country—the best on the face of the earth;
One people—and true, by adoption or birth;
One language—unspoken by tyrant or slave;
One banner—the flag of the free and the brave.
From ocean to ocean, from valley to crag:
One country, one people, one language, one flag!

by James Ball Naylor

. . . . . .

Self-Confidence

If you think that you're beaten—you're beaten,
    If you think you don't dare—well you don't;
If you think you can't win—before you begin—
    It's almost a cinch that you won't.
The victory isn't assured to
    The stronger or luckier man;
But the fellow who wins is the fellow who grins—
    And truly believes that he can!

by James Ball Naylor

. . . . . .

What Can We Do?

If you can't bear a gun
And go after the Huns,
In that bloody land over the pond,
You can loosen your collars
And earn a few dollars—
And purchase a Liberty bond.
If your hair is too white
To get into the fight,
And your legs are acquainted with cramps,
You can join the exhorters
And save up your quarters—
And buy a few little Thrift stamps.
If you can't brest the foam,
You can stay at home
And look after the hive and the honey;
You can plan, you can slave,
You can make, you can save—
And furnish the means and the money!

by James Ball Naylor

. . . . . .

Old McGuffey's

Old McGuffey's! Old McGuffey's!
How we used to read 'em through,
When the sun of youth was shinin'
And the flowers drenched with dew.
Now the autumn winds are whistlin'——
All our memories to mock;
And the frost is on our punkin——
Which gives fader quite a shock!

by James Ball Naylor

· · · · · ·

The Tan Shoe Gang

Now what's all this rattle and clatter
        Disturbing the still summer day,
And what in the nation's the matter
        With Jamie Rusk over the way?
He frightens the kids with his squalling,
        He shoots off his mouth with a bang,
And keeps on eternally bawling:
            "The Tan
                Shoe
                    Gang!"

He ridicules shoes that are decent
        And starts out the mischief to raise,
He objects to a shirt that is "recent"—
        His own shirt "has seen better days!"
And a pair of clean hose! He can't bear 'em:
        It gives the old duffer a pang
Just to see a few GENTLEMEN wear 'em—
            The Tan
                Shoe
                    Gang!

He says—and he says it so warmly
    One would think 'twere a voice from on high,--
That the Demmies of Morgan downed Gormley;
    What a dose of political lye!
One can tell a wild ass by his braying,
    One can tell a cracked bell by its clang,
And can class Jamie Rusk by his saying:
    "The Tan
        Shoe
            Gang!"

Has it come to this pass in old Morgan,
    That men who are honest and clean
Must bow down to the triple-faced Gorgon
    Of jealousy, heartless and mean?
Must these men be forever assailed with
    The most vapid and witless of slang,
And be crucified daily and nailed with—
    The Tan
        Shoe
            Gang!

Jamie Rusk, ere the campaign is over,
    Ere the dawn of election day,
This "gang" will be rolling in clover—
    And you will be "under the hay!"
And the people will be so well suited
    They won't care a tarnation dang,
Tho' you're pummeled and trampled and booted
        By The Tan
            Shoe
                Gang!

                    by J. B. N.

· · · · · ·

Snow Scene

Fairy Land—Oh, Fairy Land!
White and bright and airyland!
All the braw boughs bending low,
With the weight of the driven snow;
Winds at rest and sounds forbidden—
Song birds snugly huddled, hidden,
Where the great trees stiffly stand,
Fast asleep in Fairy Land!

Magic Land—Oh, Magic Land!
Pales and pulseless tragic land!
Every elf and fairy hid
Neath a spotless coverlid;
All the sky with gray beclouded—
All the earth in white enshrouded;
Not a bloom or bud at hand—
O'er the wastes of Magic Land!

Pixy Land—Oh, Pixie Land!
Beauteous, barren, tricksy land!
Not a fruit nor flower seen,
Not a sprout nor leaf of green;
Ne'er a beam of sunshine burning—
N'er a sign of spring returning.
Just a dead-white landscape grand—
Is the realm of Pixy Land!

by James Ball Naylor

Roller Skatin'

By jocks! Us folks in Clovertown 're strenuous these days;
The secret is we've gone an' got the roller-skatin' craze.
Each woman talks o' skates all day an' dreams of 'em in bed—
An' has eight wheels upon her feet an' sixteen in her head.
The men 're just as bad—'r worse; an' I'm right here to say
The kids 'ave all gone daffy—an' the devil is to pay!
They don't take time to read n'r write—an hardly time to think;
An' late an' soon an' night an' noon they're at the skatin'-rink.

The theatre an' lyceum ain't havin' half a trade;
The skatin' craze has come along an' laid 'em in the shade.
W'y, Rever'nd Gabfest come to town to talk, an' I declare
His audience was princip'ly big chunks of empty air;
There wasn't no one there but Stumpy Brown an' Limpy Tate—
An' half a dozen other crippled chaps that couldn't skate.
The Rever'nd intimated, with a mighty nasty wink,
Some folks was crippled in the head—an' at the skatin'-rink.

There ain't a ball n'r billiard-hall a-runnin' in the town;
An' business—it has gone 'way back, an' took to settin' down.
W'y even church an' Sunday-school 're knocked out good an' flat;
An' pennies 're so seldom it don't pay to pass the hat.
We're all so pesky strenuous that ev'ry feller feels
He hain't got time to use his head—he has to use his heels.
We pay no bills, we heed no duns; you see we need the chink
To patronize the happy chaps that run the skatin'-rink.

But—holy smoke!—of all the sports fer upright, downright fun
An' comic sights, a skatin'-rink ain't second-best to none.
Jest take 'bout forty-'leven fools, an' let 'em start to glide
Around a floor that's slicker than a jack-plane's under side,
An' you'll—well, you'll think other sports 're most too tame an' slow—
That roller skatin's purty near the whole darn circus show;
You'll look an' laugh, an' laugh an' look, an' wipe y'r eyes an' blink—
An' wish the whole big earth was jest a monster skatin'-rink.

I stood an' watched 'em 'tother night—an saw ol' Bobby Moore
Turn half a dozen summersaults before he hit the floor;
Well, that encouraged Minnie Jones, an' she went in the air
An' shot up through the rafters—an' she never touched a hair.
Then half a minute later ol' Philander Smith went lame,
An' ev'erbody piled on him—just like a football game.
When he got out he looked some like the famous missin'-link;
An' he used unseemly language 'bout the harmless skatin'-rink.

I'm doin' purty well myself—I've only tried it twice;
An' each time I was in the game—an' re'ly cut some ice.
At least I cut some didoes that was never cut before—
An' kicked out half a winder-sash some nine feet from the floor.
Yes—yes! Fer acrobats an' clowns an' gymnasts an' the rest,
A skatin'-rink is jest the place to see 'em at the'r best;
So Clovertown is happy an' is savin' up her chink,
To patronize the jolly chaps that run the skatin'-rink.

by James Ball Naylor

The Daily Paper

We've got the free delivery now—
 It goes right past our dwellin';
An' how we ever done before—
 Well, gosh! there ain't no tellin'.
Mirandy's steppin' mighty high
 An' cuttin' many a caper;
She says we're getting citified—
 We take the daily paper.

At dinner time when I come in,
 An' smell the potpie b'ilin',
Mirandy spreads the tablecloth—
 An' says to me, a-smilin':
"That ol' Japan—she's mighty slick,
 An' Rooshia can't escape 'er;
Ol' Togo' sunk the Rooshian ships—
 I seen it in the paper."

At supper-time an' milkin'-time
 She tags around behind me,
A-talkin' 'bout the daily news—
 Wherever she can find me.
It's: "Cy, they're diggin' that canal—
 A-usin' plow an' scraper;
An' Teddy's killed another bear—
 I seen it in the paper."

An' after supper when I set
    Out on the porch, a-smokin',
She'll hitch 'er chair up close to mine——
    A-chucklin' like an' chokin'
An' say: "The weather's got so kinked
    The weather-man can't shape 'er
I guess he'll have to quit his job——
    I seen it in the paper."

Well, that's the way it goes all day;
    An' when I've laid my head, sir,
Upon the piller——gone to sleep,
    She'll pop up straight in bed, sir,
An' holler: "Do you know, Cy Jones,
    A candle's called a taper?"
'R some 'tarnal thing like that!——
    "I seen it in the paper."

by James Ball Naylor

. . . . . .

You Will—And You Won't

"You will if you will,
And you won't if you won't;
You'll be damned if you do—
You'll be damned if you don't!"

The world's in a contest of faith and of doubt—
Over things the contestants know nothing about;
Whether one book of myths, of all under the sun,
Should be reckoned as true—and if so, then which one;
Whether Man barked his shins, in a long-ago fall,
And what salve he should use—if he barked 'em at all,
And it's this thing you'll credit—and this thing you won't,
And you're damned if you do—and you're damned if you don't!

Are you Buddhist, Mohammedan, lowly Hindu?
Do you think as do these? You'll be damned if you do!
Are you Catholic, Protestant? Will you or won't
You acknowledge the faith? You'll be damned if you don't!
The Christian damns everyone smeared with the tar
Of a pagan belief—so you're damned if you are;
And the Heathen damns all who are daubed with the paint
Of a contrary faith—so you're damned if you ain't!

There's a heaven somewhere, all are eager to tell—
And they're equally eager to prate of a hell;
And they argue of highway and byway and pike,

Of signboards and bridges, toll gates and the like,
Till the saint is befogged and the sinner can't make
Head nor tail of their words—as to which road to take.
So, my friend, I'd advise you to jack up your goods
And hike out 'cross the fields—and just take to the woods!

For the woods and the fields are abloom, and the birds
And the bees are on terms with the flocks and the herds;
And all nature is kind, and there's no one to tell
You to take his belief—or to go plumb to hell!
So I'll take to the woods, with my staff and my pack,
And I'll keep hiking on—and I'll never come back.
They may say I'll be damned if I don't hold their view;
Well, I'll tell 'em right here—I'll be damned if I do!

by James Ball Naylor

. . . . . .

The Hoochy-Koochy

Well, Mammy, back I be ag'in from the show in Punkinville;
An' of acr'bats, an' 'rangotangs, an' sich, I've had my fill.
I saw the monkeys an' the clowns, an' watched the whole parade;
I tagged the bands up street and down, an' heerd the tunes they played.
I took in all the side-shows, I'm sorry fer to say——
No, that ain't so; they took me in——I guess is 'bout the way.
But of all the dod-burned blistered cheats the devil ever made,
Was that hoochy-koochy feller——an' the little tune he played:

[Music]

He played it on a 'tarnal little squirt-gun of a horn;
An' it sounded like a nest of bumble-bees among the corn.
He said his show was educatin', eddifyin' an' refined——
An' jest intended to improve the morals an' the mind.
I paid ten cents an' slid right in; an, Mammy, hid y'r face
W'ile I tell you 'bout the wicked sights I saw in that there place:
Some pretty gals——with not much clo'es——was dancin' round the tent,
An' a-jigglin' an' a-wigglin' to the music as it went:

[Music]

"My dear ol' Rube," says one of 'em, in accents loud an' clear,
"You're gittin' purtier ev'ry day——an' younger ev'ry year.
Y'r whiskers is as neat an' trim, y'r shirt-front is as white;
An' then, dear Rube, y'r clo'es, you know, 're simply out o' sight.
That made me mad, my dander riz——an' I bellered out with spunk:
"Your clo'es is out o' sight, miss——fer you've left 'em in y'r trunk!"
The people whooped an' howled, you know, an' give three hearty cheers——
An' I slid out, with that 'ere tune a'ringin' in my ears:

[Music]

by James Ball Naylor

Ed Reynolds

Who ran his good train up and down?——
　　Ed Reynolds!
From Parkersburg—from Zanesville town—
　　Ed Reynolds!
Who, days and weeks, and months and years—
Who eased our burdens, dried our tears—
And always brought us smiles and cheers?—
　　Ed Reynolds!

Who knew each spike and tie and rail?—
　　Ed Reynolds!
Who knew the wag of each dog's tail?—
　　Ed Reynolds!
Who knew the lowly and the grand,
And felt this vale his native land—
And had a clasp for every hand?
　　Ed Reynolds!

And now that he must leave us—aye!—
　　Ed Reynolds!
He has a teardrop in his eye?—
　　Ed Reynolds!
And we'll be glad, where' e're the place,
Once more to see his smiling face,
And hold him in a close embrace,
　　Ed Reynolds!

by James Ball Naylor

. . . . . .

I Want to Know

Do the roses bloom in Roseville everyday?
Are the Maltese cats in Malta fond of whey?
I would also ask you whether
It is always summer weather
Down at Summerfield—and fit for making hay?

Do the crooks all come from Crookville? Let me know
Are the gay sports down at Gaysport swift or slow?
Are the folks at Pleasant City
Always singing some sweet ditty?
When they say "go" up at Sago—do they go?

Does Old Father Adam live in Adamsville?
Or has he an abode at Adams Mill?
Do the citizens all stumble
Down at Duncan Falls—and tumble?
Do they have some high old doings at High Hill?

Are the folks called well at Caldwell when they're sick?
And at Thornville—are they sharp enough to stick?
Do they gnash their teeth unduly
Up at Nashport when unruly?
If they saw war up at Warsaw would they kick?

Do they live in barns at Barnsville for a show?
Did old Noah build the Newark that we know?
    Are they strict on prohibition
    Even when they go afishin'—
Down at Waterford, they love cold water so?

Are the maidens of Belle Valley belles indeed?
Are the girls of Morgan Run renowned for speed?
    If you had it, would you bet a
    Daddy dollar Mari-ett-a
Famous high school and a college at one feed?

Do the Corning folks have corns that hurt like sin?
Do the Quaker City damsels never grin?
    But then, what's the use of tasking
    Folks with questions like I'm asking?
We're all Buckeyes—and of common blood and kin.

by James Ball Naylor

· · · · · ·

Good, Bad, and Indifferent

All men are good, all men are bad—
    When it comes to life's proprieties;
They're just like Heinz's pickles, lad—
    Fifty-seven varieties.

by JBN

. . . . . .

My Age?

I am a youth—of course I am!
    A supple youth, I ween;
I have the art, I play the part—
    A youth of 17.

But tricksy nature, mad with mirth—
    And for a bit of fun!—
Just turns the figures round-about,
    And makes me 71.

by James Ball Naylor

. . . . . .

Across the Miles

'Tis coming Christmas-time, Old Friend,
        And be it bright or drear,
Let's lift our hearts in thankfulness—
        And just be glad we're here;
Let's live and love and laugh, and face
        The world with cheery smiles;
And since we may not meet, let's now
        Shake hands across the miles!

by James Ball Naylor

. . . . . .

As English Is Pronounced

If r-o-u-g-h spells ruff
And t-o-u-g-h spells tuff,
    Is a fellow to blame
    If he happens to claim
That c-o-u-g-h spells cuff?
But—
If b-o-u-g-h spells bow,
And p-l-o-u-g-h spells plow,
    Then isn't it plain
To a thinking man's brain
That c-o-u-g-h spells cow?
And—
If t-h-r-o-u-g-h spells throo,
And s-l-o-u-g-h spells sloo,
    Is it out of the way
    For a fellow to say
That c-o-u-g-h spells coo?
Yet—
If d-o-u-g-h spells doe,
And t-h-o-u-g-h spells tho,
    Is a man far from right
    Who insists with his might
That c-o-u-g-h spells coe?
Still—
If t-r-o-u-g-h spells troff,
Why, o-u-g-h spells off:
    And it's perfectly simple,
    As plain as a pimple—
That c-o-u-g-h spells coff.

by James Ball Naylor

What is Success?

What is Success?
The rheum-eyed miser says it means
The yellow treasure that he gleans,
　　About the marts of trade;
The golden wealth that he has made
By delving deep with pick and spade—
　　All in his brass-bound caskets laid.

What is Success?
The warrior says it means to march
Beneath the great triumphal arch,
　　And wear the victor's crown;
To carve a niche with trusty sword,
In which his statue may be stored—
　　To hurl his rivals down.

What is Success?
The statesman and the scholar say
It means a wealth of verdant bay
　　Entwined about a name;
A something that, when mortal breath
Surrenders to the damps of death,
　　Is called immortal fame.

　　And thus—and thus!
Each one his definition lends—
The mighty torrent-never ends,
　　But broader, deeper grows.
You've said: "May gracious heaven bless,
And send a measure of success!"
　　Your meaning no one knows!

by James Ball Naylor

The Prognosticator

Said the barnyard cock, to his list'ning flock—
      With a squint at the weather-vane,
And his larboard eye, on the cloudless sky:
      "We are in for a spell of rain."
So he plumed and stalked—and he bragged and talked
      To his harem of speckled hens;
And he flapped and flew, and he clapped and crew
      To the clack of their shrill "amens."

And the wind blew east—but never the least
      Indication of coming rain;
And the wind blew west—'twas a juggling jest,
      To the jiggling weather-vane.
Then the wind blew south—but the dusty drouth
      It made no sign of flight;
And the wind blew north, as the last and forth—
      It had circled the compass, quite.

Squawked the barnyard flock, to the weather-cock:
      "Is our prophecy like to fail?"
But the sage old bird said never a word,
      As he veered with the shifting gale.
Then the farmer cried: "Surely some one's lied—
      And the rooster's the very one!"

Just a gurgling note, in that fool fowl's throat—
    And his reckless race was run!

    Moral
Learn a lesson plain, from the weather-vane:
    If you'd have your opinions please,
And be always right, keep your mouth shut tight—
    And veer with the vagrant breeze!

                    by James Ball Naylor

                . . . . . .

The Devil's Tea Table

O monster rock! Firm-poised it stands
Upon a base of crumbling shale;
'Twas shaped by Satan's cunning hands
In ages past—so runs the tale—
And served Hell's demons, great and small,
As table to their banquet hall,
Though countless years have rolled away,
The Devil's table stands, today,
As firm as when, with hellish glee,
The black imps held their revelry.

It seems the feeble fluttering breath
That issues from the lips of death—
The faint and fickle summer breeze
That stirs the blossoms on the trees,
Could shake the great rock's slender base
And hurl it from its resting-place;
And yet the strongest gales that sweep
Across the torrid Indian deep,
The Polar winds—the fierce cyclone—
Are all too weak—combined, alone—
To cast the monarch from its throne.

Beyond the blue Muskingum's bed
It rears its gray and wrinkled head;
Though aged, still erect—sublime.
It gazes on the march of time,
And towers above the verdant sod,
A monolith of nature's God.
When years on years have hurried past
Until God's dial marks the last;
Oh! may the grim old rock still keep
Its vigil on the stony steep.

by James Ball Naylor

• • • • • •

This monstor rock was located three miles north of McConnelsville, Ohio. When viewed up close it appeared to lean in whatever direction from which it was viewed. On July 1, 1906, it toppled.

Some Machine

If you have a thirst for travel,
 Time will bring you your reward;
If you cannot own an auto——
 You can surely own a Ford.
You can scorch across the country,
 Like a hand-car——till you balk;
If you want to travel faster——
 You can climb right out and walk.
  You can climb right out and walk!

If your old farm mare's too speedy,
 Turn 'er out to earn 'er board;
"Safety First" should be your motto——
 Sell a hog and buy a Ford.
You can practice on suggestions——
 Think you're flying, if you will;
Though you have to push on up-grades,
 You can always ride down hill.
  You can always ride down hill!

If you have a grain of gumption
 Packed away within your gourd,
Rob the baby's bank some Sunday——
 And on Monday buy a Ford.
You can have the fun of cranking
 From the mountains to the coast;
Then, when you are tired of working,
 Send it home by parcel-post.
  Send it home by parcel-post!

by James Ball Naylor

Truth Will Prevail

"The earth's a globe, and every day
    Turns over!" Bruno said.
They bound him to a fiery stake—
    And Bruno joined the dead.
The priesthood had its way and will—
    But, lo, the earth's rotating still!

Brave Galileo said: "The earth
    Goes circling round the sun."
They threw him into prison—
    And they thought the matter done.
The bigots had their will and way—
    But the earth goes round the sun today!

The governor of Tennessee
    Said, "Evolution's fraught
With danger—and such heresy
    Shall not be voiced nor taught!"
W-e-ll, he may work his will and way—
    But evolution's here to stay!

The clerical may wring his hands
    And show himself unnerved,
Because his fallacies are not
    Respected and preserved.
But, one by one, they pass—they're gone;
    And truth comes calmly marching on!

by James Ball Naylor

A Rational Prayer

— Let me not long to be wealthy; rather let me aspire to be worthy.

— Let me not despise wealth; but let me not worship it.

— Teach me that the milled rim of the twenty-dollar gold piece is not necessarily the horizon of the universe.

— Make me thoroughly understand, and lead me to act upon the knowledge, that sixty seconds make a minute, one hundred cents make a dollar, and sixteen ounces make a pound.

— Inspire me not only to live and let live—but to live and help to live.

— Don't permit a troubled conscience to be my comrade through the day, or vain regrets to occupy my bed with me at night.

— Let me be able honestly to look the whole world in the face—and have the manly courage to tell it to go chase itself.

— Enable me so to live that I may not lose my self respect.

— See to it that I aspire to be a square man—rather than an all-round good fellow.

——*Let me earn my meal-ticket by the sweat of my own brow or the cellular vibrations of my own brain.*

—— *Deafen me not to the enticing jingle of the dirty dollar.*

—— *Relieve me not of my burdens——but make me strong and patient to bear my burdens.*

—— *Free me not from duties and responsibilities——but strengthen my resolution and add to my courage.*

——*Let me so live daily and hourly that my good wife may have and hold confidence in me, admire me, respect me, and love me, and that little children will sit upon my lap and prattle to me.*

—— *Enable me in all ways to be a MAN.*

by James Ball Naylor

· · · · · ·

The Horrid Men

Who once made women wear big hoops?
    The men!
Hoopskirts as big as chicken-coops?
    The men!
Who made 'em wear the bustle, too,
The Mother Hubbard, peek-a-boo—
That was so easy to see through?
    The men—the naughty men!

Who made 'em wear the Grecian bend?
    The men!
And drag a train that had no end?
    The men!
Who forced the Dolly Varden style,
That could be seen and heard a mile—
And made the wide world widely smile?
    The men—the cruel men!

Who now controls the weaker sex?
    The men!
And wear their waists cut in a "V,"
And have their skirts up to the knee,

And sport silk stockings? Hullee-gee!
      The men—the brutal men!

Who makes 'em wear such high-heeled shoes?
      The men!
And Summer furs? Just the news.
      The men!
Who makes the poor things bob their hair,
And paint and powder—I declare!—
Until, meek slaves, they're in despair?
      The men—the heartless men!
Who ought to be ashamed?—God wot!
      The men!
But who—I muchly fear!—are not?
      The men!
Who ought to be condemned to die—
And in a future state to fry
Throughout the endless by-and-by?
      The men—the horrid men!

            by James Ball Naylor

. . . . . .

O-hi-O

It's uncultured to boast—it's offensive, almost!
  But of all the grand states in this nation,
Just one commonwealth blest,—and the chiefest and best!—
  Gets and merits the Lord's approbation.
Why, there's not a pretext for its folks to get vexed
  'Bout the brand of weather—or scared or perplexed;
If they don't get it one day they get it the next—
  In this God-favored spot of creation!
    And the name of this state?
    Well, my lad, it's a riddle
    As slick as the top
    Of your grandmother's griddle;
    It's round at both ends
    And it's high in the middle.
    What's that? Lad, you're right!
    It's O-hi-O

Yes, it's round at each end—jolly wheels, lad, to bend
    The old commonwealth swift locomotion;
And the center we count a spring seat paramount—
    And the shrine of each statesman's devotion.
Why, our folks are so great the political slate
    Is scratched full of our names, and the pencil of Fate
Writes the name of a president down while you wait;
    We are famous from ocean to ocean!
        And the name of this state?
        Yes, my lad, it's a riddle
        As hard to make out
        As the make of a fiddle;
        It's round at both ends
        And it's high in the middle.
        Ho-ho! Right you are!
        It's O-hi-O

We're the favored of God—we're the salt of the sod!
    And the sun never sets—but just travels
Round the rim of our land, and a number-one brand
    Of the flossiest sunshine unravels.
Why, our wealth is so great we just count it by weight;
    Yea, and market our greenbacks by bundle and crate—
And from river to lake, and all over our state
    Precious stones are as common as gravel!
      And the name of this state?
      Ah, my lad, it's a riddle
      As slick as the top
      Of your grandmother's griddle;
      It's round at both ends
      And it's high in the middle.
      Ha-ha! Right you are!
      It's O-hi-O

            by James Ball Naylor

· · · · · ·

Nature

You may prate of dear, old Mother Nature,
And acclaim her as gracious and kind:
You may think she's the Earth's legislature—
But I haven't that thought in my mind.

Why, Nature's a tricksy young maiden—
Disapprove the assertion who can;
The world is her lunch-basket laden—
And the hole in the doughnut is Man!

by James Ball Naylor

· · · · · ·

Song of Malta

(Malta, the smaller of the two villages of Malta and McConnelsville
had her streets paves first. The following poem was sung at a
minstrel show.)

Oh, they say that old McConnelsville is ailing;
That she's subject to the jimjams and the jerks,
That her brain is all on fire,
And her ferver's mounting higher,
And she's having trouble with her waterworks;
That her alley-ways and passages are awful—
Her condition's never better, always worse—
'T won't be but a little while 'till they'll phone for Allie Pyle,
And they'll say, just please to bring around the hearse.

CHORUS:
> For old Malta is a high bred dandy!
> She's got paved streets and they come mighty handy,
> Good for bicycle, buggy or sleigh,
> Winter or summer—for they're built that way.
> I'm proud of my home city—
> Old McConnelsville I pity.
> Along this line she can't outshine
> This old home town of mine.

Now old Malta is as frisky as a kitten
And as buxom as a billy goat you see
For she's not a care to vex her,
For her streets are paved as nice as they can be.
She's a darling, she's a daisy, she's a dumpling,
She's molassas, she is sugar, she is sweet—
But just step across the river
And your spine will twist and shiver
As you take a look along up Center street.

CHORUS:
          For old Malta is a high bred dandy!
          She's got paved streets and they come mighty handy,
          Good for bicycle, buggy or sleigh,
          Winter or summer—for they're built that way.
          I'm proud of my home city—
          Old McConnelsville I pity.
          Along this line she can't outshine
          This old home town of mine.

                    by Dr. James Ball Naylor

                    · · · · · ·

Fate's Ultimate Plan

'Tis Fate's ultimate plan
To put on us a ban!
To go wrong, if we must—
To go right, if we can;
But who never goes wrong
Is a god, not a man.

If you err not—alas!
You're no part of the mass
Of Humanity, friend,
And we'll nod as we pass;
But you're little to me—
For you're out of my class.

by James Ball Naylor

. . . . . .

What Are You?

I'm for America—through and through!
I'm for the old Red-White-and-Blue—
Ready to serve and give and do.
I'm an American!
          What-are-you?

                by James Ball Naylor

. . . . . .

Boosting the World

I'm boosting the world on its way,
Don't shirk—with a frown on your brow;
          Get under the load,
          Or get out of the road—
And let somebody lift that knows how.

                by J. B. N.

. . . . . .

William Weil Will Wed A Widow

(Headline in Chicago Journal of Commerce)

William Weil will wed; he's got
Wads of wit, knows what is what;
Wants no wanton, wasteful, giddy.
William Weil will wed a widdy!

by J. B. N.

. . . . . .

Would Wood Saw Wood

Wood saw a wood-saw,
Now Wood would have a wood-saw that would saw
wood.
So Wood said to Wood: "If that wood-saw would
saw wood, I, Wood, would saw wood. But would that
wood-saw saw wood? Not unless Wood would saw that
wood-saw for and back on the wood, would that wood-saw saw
wood for Wood."
Yes, Wood saw that wood-saw would not saw wood,
unless Wood would saw wood with the wood-saw.
Consequently, Wood saw the wood-saw; but Wood
sawed no wood with the wood-saw.

by J. B. N.

Skat

The puppy squatted on the floor,
His mistress rushed him through the door;
She struck him with a paper—whack!
But still he left a sprinkled track
Of moisture—dampness, rather wet—
The sixteenth part of the alphabet.

by J. B. Naylor

· · · · · ·

Short Bits
by James Ball Naylor

You may boast of your ancestors, early and late;
But the question that dawns on my view
Isn't what do you think of your forebears great?
But what would <u>they</u> think of <u>you</u>?

. . . . . .

Mine vife sthood on der pavement schlick.
I cannot understand it;
First she schumped up into der air—
Und den, py gosh, she landet!

. . . . . .

Every worm beneath the moon
Draws different threads,
And late or soon
Spins, toiling out his own cocoon.

. . . . . .

Americans will fight and fall,
Arise and fight the more;
They've lost full many a battle,
But they've never lost a war.

. . . . . .

The Christian oft improves upon
The Heathen's cruel trend:
The Indian scalps his enemy—
The White Man skins his friend.

. . . . . .

The good God reigneth over all—
    And does it with impartial touch;
But when it comes to our rainfall—
    The good God raineth too darn much!
    . . . . . .

On the road to Pride-and-Pelf,
    Stands this ancient signpost:
"Every fellow for himself—
    And the devil take the hindmost!"
    . . . . . .

Said the Devil to the liar—
    As he made the heat less fervent
And withdrew him from the fire:
    "Well done, good and faithful servant!"
    . . . . . .

'Twas hash at the boarding-house every day;
And the meek boarder looked at his plate
And solemnly muttered in husky tones:
    "Hebrews, XIII-8."
    . . . . . .

The melon-colic days are come,
    The saddest of the year;
The doctor's at the sick-room door—
    The undertaker's near.
    . . . . . .

Whether we live at peace or at war,
Whether our flags be furled or unfurled,
Let us remember our old Uncle Sam
Simply can't wet-nurse the whole darn world!

. . . . . .

He that knows not, and knows not that he knows not,
  Is a dunce—without a doubt;
He that knows not, and knows he knows not,
  Is unfortunate—help him out;
He that knows, and knows not that he knows,
  Is a beggar—born to wait;
He that knows, and knows that he knows—
  Is the master of his fate!

. . . . . .

Editor's Special Selections
Written by
James Ball Naylor

I have selected a number of special poems to add to this volume. Because they show the broad spectrum of Naylor's ability while adding his personal and emotional touch, I feel they are especially fitting for this volume that Lucile dedicated as a tribute to her father.

Theresa Marie Flaherty

The Muskingum Valley in southeastern Ohio was home to James Ball Naylor for his entire life. Its beauty was extolled in many of his poems. As a boy, he spent long hours outdoors exploring its wonders, and as a country doctor, he traveled its dusty roads on horseback or in a horse drawn buggy. During those long, lonely rides, ideas for poems and stories were born as his horse plodded along. This poem, his first published poem, won the ten dollar first prize at the Morgan County Fair in 1889 and appeared in a local paper on August 24th, 1889. Over the years, he made various changes to several lines, and the poem appeared in different publications, as well as in his own Book of Buckeye Verse.

The Muskingum Valley

There's a valley that lies midst verdure-crowned hills,
    And a beautiful river flows through it;
This river was fed by the most sparkling rills,
    In the days when the Redman first knew it;
    And these children of nature gazed into its reach
Reflecting the blue of the sky,
    And gave it the name, in their guttural speech,
Of Muskingum, which means the "Moose Eye."

The lodge of the Delaware stood on its shore,
    And his fragile canoe cut its foam;
His sinewy arm flied the light ashen oar,
    As he stemmed the fierce current near home;
While back in the forest where flowers were out,
    And the sweetest of perfumes did blow,

The cliff and the hill-side re-echoed the shout,
    Of the copper-hued children below.

At night when the council-fire blazed on the scene,
    And mirrored itself in the waves,
The beech and the elm shook their branches of green
    O'er the heads of the Indian braves;
The war-whoop that rang through the shadowy glade,
    Was answered from hill-top and flood;
The red, painted forms in the war-dance were swayed,
    As they acted their orgies of blood.

The bear and the deer had a home in the wood,
    While beautiful fish filled the stream;
The bald-eagle soared where the giant oak stood,
    And sounded his merciless scream;
The Sun, as he came from the civilized East,
    Peeped into the beautiful vale
And found it the land of wild man and wild beast,
    And unknown to the emigrant's trail.

Dame Nature was here in her primitive state;
    But the time was drawing a pace,
When the sons of New England would settle a date
    To soften the look on her face.
For an emigrant's barge was then on its way—
    Where the mighty Ohio sweeps down—
Whose owners would land at no distant day
    And establish the germ of a town.

Just where the Muskingum empties its flood
    Is the site that these pioneers chose;
And, with hopes of the future to temper their blood.
    They felt little fear of their foes.
Soon the blue smoke curled high from the cabin of logs,
    And the settler's axe rang keen and clear;
Soon the crack of his rifle, the bark of his dogs,
    Sent a chill to the heart of the deer.

Thenceforward the Red Man's fate was decreed—
    He must vacate the land of his birth;
For the Pale-face, obeying his nature and need,
    Was clearing and tilling the earth.
But the proud aboriginal's heart was on fire—
    And many fierce combats were fought;
Oft the settler's log hut was his funeral pyre—
    For with blood this fair valley was bought.

Lo, the many-hued cycle of years had revolved—
    And the whole panorama is changed!
The problem of which race should conquer is solved;
    And the hills that the Indian ranged
Are dotted with farmhouses, cosy and white;
    While the green tassled corn waves the air,
Or the fire on some hearth gleams rosy and bright,
    Where the ravenous beast made his lair.

A hamlet now stands where the wigwam of bark
    Once nestled among the huge trees;
The fire of the furnace illumines the dark
    And the black smoke is borne on the breeze,
Where—many moons past—the tired warrior wound
    A blanket about his great form
And, throwing himself on the hard-frozen ground,
    Sought slumber, protected and warm.

The "Moose Eye" rolls down from the North as of old;
    But its current is hindered and stayed,
By the Pale-face's will and his works manifold—
    Such dams as the beaver ne'er made.
No dugout canoe on its surface now floats—
    The soft dip of the paddle is still;
But the echoes are waked by the puff of the boats
    And the whirring of wheels at the mill.

Today, as the morning sun visits our land,
    It smiles on a beautiful scene:
A river that flowing o'er glittering sand,
    Is fringed by a border of green;
A broad, level bottom-land stretching away
    Is burdened with good golden grain—
And acre on acre of sweet-smelling hay
    Is kissed by the dew and the rain.

The serpentine track of the railway is here—
    And the pulsating engine speeds by;
Its screech as it passes rings savage and clear,
    Far back on the cliffs gray and high.
The time-tested popular leans over the brink
    Of the rock-girdled summit it's on;
And the wild fox steals down to the river to drink
    As it did in the days that are gone.

. . . . . .

Naylor was a wonderful versifier. His ability to compose a poem on a moment's notice was well known. Though such verses might not withstand critical analysis, they did illustrate his quick wit and keen sense of humor. One such example is his delightful response to a letter he received from Victoria, Australia. in April, 1903:

Dear Mr. Naylor:

Would you do an Australian girl the very great favor to send her your autograph and excuse her trespassing on your good nature to that extent.——Fame has its penalties and this is one of them.

Mildred Stephenson

Naylor replied with this poem and placed his autograph at the end:

Malta, Ohio
May 13, 1903

My Dear Miss Stephenson:

If I remember,
When we have June you have December;
In other words, 'tis winter there
When we have summer bright and fair.
So now, perhaps, while we are roasting
In summer's heat, you may be "coasting;"
(A vagrant guess! More like, the word
That names the sport, you've never heard.

If so, it is a burning shame;
But then, my dear, you're not to blame.)
Or, clad in garments warm and nice,
Are you skimming o'er the crystal ice.
(You <u>do</u> have ice—this fact I know;
My cyclopedia tells me so.)
Heighho! I've drifted quite away
From what I really meant to say.

'Twas this: I'm please—therefore, this smile!—
To think you deemed it worth your while
To send a letter o'er the sea,
To Yankeeland, a begging me
To send to you—there, there, don't laugh!
My wretched, scrawly autograph.
(My dear, it wouldn't bring a peck
Of gold, if scribbled on a check!)

But here it is; and may it please
The gods of Antipodes
To bear it far o'er sea and land
And place it safely in your hand.

P.S.

Fair stranger, pardon this poor verse;
I <u>can't</u> write better—<u>can</u> write worse.

All anger, therefore, promptly quell —
And thank your stars I've done so well!

Sincerely yours,

James Ball Naylor

. . . . . .

On another occasion, Naylor received a request for an autograph from an enterprising collector from Vineyard Haven, Massachusetts while the valley was recovering from flooding—either in 1898 or 1913. He remarked in print, "Now authors' and journalists' autographs have little value when used to substantiate a check; but they do possess a modicum of value—in the estimation of certain unconventional souls!—when used to grace a collection." So he sent his autograph with the poem below. He added, "I haven't heard from my compatriot yet; but I'm expecting the check. And when it comes I'll turn it over to our relief committee, with the keenest pleasure. If there are others who would like to exchange autographs with me, on the same delectable terms—well, I'm open for business."

Come Across With The Cash

The flood has come, the flood has gone—
Of worldly gear we are bereft;
But still I send my autograph—
The only one that I have left.
And since the flood has come and gone—
And left our town a sorry wreck,
I'd like to get your autograph—
Appended to a goodly check.

· · · · · ·

Naylor was keenly interested in politics from an early age. This no doubt stems from losing his father in the Civil War and gaining a stepfather who survived it. He ventured into the political arena as a candidate on several occasions. After his last unsuccessful bid for the Ohio Senate in 1910, he wrote this clever poem that he sent to those patients that owed on their accounts, promising to leave the political arena, admitted his dire financial situation and, in a most pleasant manner, asked them all to pay.

A Plea and a Promise

Election day has come and gone—
And gone, too, are my hopes;
For Fate gave me a final punch—
And knocked me through the ropes.

My chances and my pocketbook
Together went to smash;
And so I'm out of politics—
And, also, out of cash.

Old Winter's knocking at my door;
And in the dismal dawn
He whistles through the keyhole: "Son,
Where has all your money gone?"

And when I open not to him,
He rattles at my sash
And shrieks: "Your bills are overdue;
You've got to raise some cash!"

Kind friend, if you will come around
And pay your meager score,
I pledge my word to you I'll be
A candidate no more.

My head has felt the fist of Fate,
My back, Misfortune's lash;
I need your sympathy, good friend—
Likewise, I need your cash.

From this day forth I'll minister
Unto my neighbor's ills,
Nor meddle much with politics—
I'll simply pedal pills;

I'll try to serve all faithfully—
This is no promise rash.
So come around and shake my hand—
And leave a little cash.

. . . . . .

Naylor first wrote under the nom de plume of S. Q. Lapius, a play on the name of the roman god of healing, Esculapius. By 1900, he dropped the pseudonym and became consistent in using his full name, James Ball Naylor, to identify his work. Thus, his very early works are easily identified. Using his pseudonym, he wrote "Call the Roll," a poem of political significance, dealing with the sudden disappearance of the names of a number of Democratic Congressmen from the House roll. The poem was copied in a number of exchanges and made the rounds of the press without credit being given to Naylor. In a number of papers, it appeared as though original material. The editor of the Herald in McConnelsville, Ohio, called the poem, "not only ably written but contained many palpable hits, and showed that the author was well versed in the characteristics of public men." Characteristics, apparently, that continue to this day.

Call the Roll

Missing, missing—O! my soul—
Mark the missing, call the roll.
"Mr. Outhwaite of Ohio!"
Wraithly voices answer—"hence,"
And the tomcat squalls—"Mariah"
Up and down the alley fence.
Fateful ides of drear November
Long will Democrats remember.
"Tom L. Johnson!" At the call
Winterstorm clouds like a pall

Gather in the northern sky,
And the bleak winds speeding by
Shriek a word and hurry on.
By old Grover's best Havana—
By Pap Thurman's red bandanna—
Men and brethren, he is "gone!"
Think, Oh! think the cash it cost 'im—
Can it be that we have lost 'im?
Let him go, then: call another
Stalwart friend and faithful brother.

"Objector Holman!" At the name
Surely every trump of fame
In triumphant voice will tell—
"Holman liveth, all is well!"
Nay, a thousand paper mallets
In the shape of Watson ballots
Beat him silly—beat him sore—
Worthy Holman is no more.

"Shout for Bynum, search for Bland,
Scour the woods on every hand!"
Ah! we find them face to face
Locked in one last fond embrace;
Lovers always, lovers ever,
Even death could not dissever.
Bynum sowed his free-trade wheat,
Reaped he tares and sad defeat;
Bland, the honest, Bland, the bold,

Cared for neither fame nor gold—
Only silver caught his eye
In the happy days gone by.
Rest ye, comrades, sleep amain—
We shall greet ye ne'er again.

"Men and brethren, leave off kissing
Those dead faces—hunt the missing!"
Look for Cummings, Wilson, Hatch—
Lasso Bryan—try to catch
Some brief note from that sweet singer,
Crisp's beloved—Chairman Springer.
Where, Oh! where is Sockless Jerry,
Pracy, Stevens, Pence and Heard?
Sound the tocsin, warriors, hurry—
Bring us back one hopeful word!

Missing, missing—one and all!
Dead, or lost beyond recall.
By old Grover's best Havana—
By Pap Thurman's red bandanna—
Though we weep and wail and whoop,
Brethern, we are in the soup!

· · · · · ·

Naylor was a frequent contributor of poetry, political and otherwise, to the Ohio State Journal and knew the editors well. They remarked in print: "When our dear friend, James Ball Naylor, of the Marion Star, approves of anything we say, he calls us an Ohio newspaper; and when he doesn't, he mentions our name—usually adding that we have been a Democrat and a free-trader from our youth up.—Ohio State Journal. Naylor responded with:

The Why Of It

When I approve I name you not,
Because I know 'twould make you hot—
Such wondrous modesty you've got;
But when I disapprove and flout,
I must not leave good folks in doubt—
I've got to name and point you out.
Believe me, Bob, for it is true:
It hurts me more than it does you—
My heart's so tender, through and through!

· · · · · ·

By the time Franklin Roosevelt's New Deal was in the process of being implemented between 1933 and 1936, Naylor had lost his twin grandsons. During the dark days and months after this loss, he lost a lot of his drive and his writing days were limited. He had not lost his political fervor, however. Naylor took a poem that he had written earlier, titled The Elephant and the Tiger (page 70), and reworked a few lines, giving it political significance.

The Elephant and The Jackass

The elephant and the jackass met
        Within a woodland cool;
The jackass saw his mangy hide
        Reflected in a pool;
Yet, being vain and frivolous,
        Remarked with caustic wit:
"My dear old fashioned rube, your clothes
        Are sadly a misfit.
Your trousers bag about the knees,
        Your coat is quite too loose,
                Your lack of style
                Is simply vile—
And merits no excuse."

The Elephant, good naturedly, replied:
"My New Deal dude,
I must admit my garments are
Old fashioned, quite, and rude;
But still I would not swap with you,
Though you should offer boot;
I do not care to own or wear
A ragged New Deal suit.
However, you had better leave;
I might, in sudden spunk—
Denude your back
And deftly pack
Your carcass in my truck!"

. . . . . .

During World War 1 Naylor wrote patriotic verse and had cards printed that revealed his sentiments. He sold the cards, when he did not give them away, for a few pennies, a nickel or a dime and donated the money to organizations helping the service men—such as the Red Cross and the Salvation Army. The poem refers to Kaiser Wilhelm 11, Germany's last Kaiser, who was the Commander in Chief of the German armed forces throughout the war.

I'd Rather Be Afloat and Alone

I'd rather be afloat and alone,
On a sea of blood, in a boat of stone;
With sails of iron and oars of lead,
And a frowning midnight sky o'erhead;
With the wrath of God for a wrecking gale—
And hell for a port toward which to sail;
Than ship on a dreadnaught staunch and new—
With Kaiser Bill and his pirate crew!

. . . . . .

In 1907, Naylor was invited as the guest of honor at a banquet of the Harrow Club in Columbus, Ohio. The club had only ten members, and meetings were very interesting events as there were no rules or regulations. Invitations were greatly prized. Naylor was one of nine guests invited. His good friend Harry Westerman was the master of ceremonies. Naylor was the principal entertainer, but several others spoke honoring him, including Samuel Flickinger, one of the first editors to receive Naylor's poems. Another of the guests, Charles Kinney, read a poem that he wrote dedicated to Naylor, and Colonel Wilson of the Ohio State Journal, added to his accolades.

Another well known member of the club was Opha Moore, an Ohio historian, to whom Naylor penned the following poem when he could not attend an upcoming meeting:

My dear Opha Moore:

I am taking
In the strenuous effort of making
You fellows up there understand:
That the railroads now issue no passes,
That they've called in the ones that I've had,
That the highways are glue and molasses—
And the walking's infernally bad.

However, I'm herewith remitting
A check for five dollars, to rub
Out my part of the cost of your sitting—
And to pay for my share of the grub;

So reserve me a peg in the hallway—
        A mere hook for my battered old hat,
Just to show to your friend, in a small way,
        That you miss him—wherever he's <u>at</u>.

And when duly assembled at table,
        Kindly designate one empty chair
And indulge in the fanciful fable
        That your rhyme-jingling brother is there;
Place a plate for the poor luckless sinner,
        Who begs your indulgence to say
That he always enjoys a good dinner—
        But not in this long-distance way.

And, also, when eating and drinking,
        And laughing and chatting in glee,
Waste a wee fleeting moment in thinking
        Of him who is absent—that's me:
And should some fellow chance to unravel
        A yarn of rare worth, bear in mind
That this dull Harrow tooth scratching gravel
        Has a fondness for that very kind.

In Conclusion, when dinner is over
        And the old Harrow's ripping around—
Making paths through the blossomy clover
        And leaving its marks on the ground,
Should some fellow get hurt in the frolic,—
        Wherever that region may be!-

And give him red-pepper sauce, for the colic—
   And charge him two dollars for me.

And I'm wishing—though some in doubt whether
   I can make it quite plain in my rhyme—
That you'll have, when you all get together,
   Just a hell of a Harrowing time!
And if stern Duty wasn't my jailer—
   But there—there! I know it can't be!
So I sign myself—
   Yours,
      James Ball Naylor.

P.S. Save a stogie for me!

. . . . . .

Although Naylor himself did not drive, he did own several cars over the years. This poem conveys his delight and satisfaction with his Studebaker Commander.

Ode to a Commander

I COMMAND
I command the miles to shorten—and they <u>do</u>.
I command the landscape to fall behind me—"like an ocean flying before the wind"—and it <u>obeys</u>.
I command the hills to flatten and disappear—and they <u>heed</u>.
I command smiles to replace frowns—and my word is <u>law</u>.
I command weariness and worry to seek oblivion, and pleasure and happiness to come in their stead—and my will <u>prevails</u>.
I am "The Commander."
I have been weighed in the balance of service, and I have not been found <u>wanting</u>.
I have been tried out in every way, and have come through every test triumphant!
I am the <u>car of cars!</u>
I am The Studebaker Commander!

. . . . . .

Over the years, Naylor met and became friends with other well known authors, poets and politicians, many of whom also participated on the Lyceum and Chautauqau circuits. In his later years, he exchanged books with other authors— each inscribing and autographing the books they exchanged. Naylor's library contained many such treasures. Irvng Bacheller, author of Eben Holden, sent him a copy of his latest book, D'ri and I, with the following autograph written in it: "Dr. James Ball Naylor, with compliments and good wishes, Irving Bacheller." In return Naylor sent Bacheller a copy of his Sign of the Prophet with the following verse:

This greeting from the West I send:
    My fate's best gifts befall you!
I'd like to name you as my friend—
    If that would not appall you.

I make no claim to match your flight—
    You've soared to fame, as few do;
You would not write the tales I write--
    I could not write those you do.

But yet as stories are the rage--
    And some one must indite 'em,
May kindly providence engage
    That you and I may write 'em.

· · · · · ·

On a visit to Dayton, Ohio, my husband and I visited Dunbar House, the home of Paul Dunbar, poet laureate of African Americans, another well known author with whom Naylor exchanged books. There on a bookshelf, we recognized one of Naylor's novels, one of several printed with a distinctive red cover. Naylor also sent Dunbar a copy of his Golden Rod and Thistle Down in exchange for the copy of Dunbar's Candle-Lightin' Time. Naylor inscribed it with the following poem:

My dear Dunbar: I wish to say
    I've read your rhythmic jingles;
And with the chime of word and rhyme,
    The ear of mem'ry tingles.

So in return for what I've had--
    A pleasure most divine, sir!
I mail to you--good hale to you!--
    This little book of mine, sir.

A forward act! No argument
    Of mine shall e'er defend it:
Yet—callow youth I am, forsooth!—
    I'm ready still to send it.

And this my hope: That you may find
    some bit of idle rhyme, sir,
With the book, to cheer your look,
    At "Candle-lightin' Time," sir!

· · · · · ·

Long before he began exchanging books and meeting fellow poets and authors, he wrote the following poem.

Some Fellers That I'd Like to Meet

The fellers that I'd like to meet
      Ain't kings an' chaps o' high degree;
Them ain't the folks I'd like to greet—
      They somehow don't appeal to me.
There's lots o' fellers, East and West,
      I've met, an' knowed, an' liked—an' yet,
The ones I know an' like the best
      Is fellers that I've never met.

The fellers that I'd like to meet?
      Well, there's Jim Riley—bless my soul!
I'd like to hear that chap repeat
      His piece 'bout that "Ol' Swimmin' Hole"!
W'y, I was in that hole with him,
      W'en we was youngsters, years ago—
Though out in hoosierdom lived Jim,
      An' I was here in O-hi-o!
I'd like to take the train some day
      Fer "Griggsby's Station"—me an' him!
An' potter 'long the hot highway,
      To "Ol' Aunt Mary's"—me an' him!
Then lollin' 'mong the orchard trees—
      An' hand in hand an' hearts in tune,

An, list'nin' to the birds an' bees—
    Jest soak ourselves "Knee-Deep in June"!

Then, 'way down South, a feller dwells—
    I'd like to take him by the hand,
An' tell him how my ol' heart swells
    With his sweet "Songs from Dixie-Land."
Jest like to tell him, o'er a pipe,
    I find his verses, more an' more,
Like Georgy melons—big an' ripe,
    An' sweet an' juicy to the core!

I s'pect his folks once wore the Gray—
    I know my folks once wore the Blue;
But them sad times has passed away—
    There's better work fer us to do!
Though he's down South, an' I'm up North,
    There ain't no reason we should fuss;
The ol' flag's ripplin' back an' forth—
    An smilin' peace down on us!

There's heaps o' chaps I'd like to meet—
    Joe Lincoln, Nixon Waterman;
A pair o' singers true an' sweet—
    An' both built on the proper plan.
I love Joe's song o' "Sunset Land,"
    An' Nixon's "Ol'-Time Quiltin' Bee"—
I'd like to tell 'em both, first-hand,
    Jest what the'r sweet songs means to me!

Of course there's other fellers—say!
    I've fancied I could tell a lie;
But I give up to Holman Day—
    There ain't no use fer me to try!
I wonder where he spins the yarn—
    In what dark corner of his brain—
To knit an' weave them fishy, darn,
    Ridic'lous tales 'bout folks in Maine!

There ain't no use to name 'em all—
    But there's that warbler, Paul Dunbar;
His banjo-tinklins' melt an' fall—
    Like music drippin' from a star.
I like "The Poet and His Song,"
    An' "When Malindy Sings" is fine;
An' then my soul goes prancin' 'long—
    Astride o' "Dat Ol' Mare o' Mine"!

I'd like to meet 'em, great an' small—
    The chaps whose jingles I 'ave read;
I'd like to meet the livin', all—
    An' them that's numbered with the dead!
Well, one sweet thought brings comfort now
    Some day I'll leave the haunts of men,
An' in that land somewhere—somehow,
    I'll maybe git to meet them then!

. . . . . .

Some of Naylor's most tender-hearted poems were early poems written about his children. Although very little of his poetry can be attributed to his later years, the following two poems, one about a visit by three of his granddaughters and another enclosed with a note to his twin grandsons when they were young, reveals him as a tender-hearted grandfather.

Three Little Girls

Three little girls came giggling down
All the way from Chicago town;
And romped and played—and blessed my days
With their ready smiles and artless ways.

Three little girls packed up and left—
And my heart is sad and my home bereft!—
But this hope remains—and will ne'er depart!—
That they'll soon come back to my home and heart!

. . . . . .

Note to Grandsons

Here are two crisp, clean dollar bills—
    One for each little Laddie.
Do you know whom they come from? Sure!
    They come from Bampy-Daddie!
For Bampy-Daddie was a boy
    One time—It does seem funny!—
And when he was, he'd like to have had
    A little spending money.

. . . . . .

In 1942, Naylor received a request for a poem about toads from Miss Lillyan Stewart, of Waycross, Georgia. For the previous eleven years, Waycross had celebrated the third week in March as "Protect the Toad Week." School children made posters, write stories and essays in the hopes of saving the toad from extinction. Naylor, intrigued by the challenge, sat down and wrote this poem. Miss Stewart responded, "What great talent you have—and you so generously share it with us. God bless you and keep you and those you love."

My Friends, The Toads

I'm eighty-one—and some folks say:
"You're growing old, you're getting gray."
But I sing on—as I have sung
Since I was very, very young.
I've roamed the woods, I've scoured the fields
And garnered much that nature yields;
I've loved the wild life, gathered flowers,
And spent full many happy hours.

My earnest mother often said—
With wagging finger, nodding head:
"My son, your mother understands
That you'll get warts upon your hands,
If dire temptation ever goads
You on to play with ugly toads."
I listened to the voice I heard—
And acted like I'd heed each word.

But as I trudged bypaths and roads,
I loitered, stopped, and played with toads;
And I can prove, in boyhood's court.
I never got a single wart.
The red head bruiser of our band
Had half a dozen on each hand;
And was admired by all the girls
With rosy cheeks and dancing curls.

Howe'er, I had small need to pine;
I had one toad that was all mine.
He hopped across our hummocked lawn,
And gorged himself from dusk 'till dawn.
I fed him fireflies all aflame—
And thought it quite a proper game;
And I? I swelled with boyish pride—
To show him lighted up inside.

. . . . . .

Naylor had a way of reflecting on simple aspects of life and capturing the essence within a few lines. This poem is a great example of that.

Life Tides

I knew him as a lusty lad—
  A few short years ago;
But now he is a grave granddad,
  Thus do the life tides flow!

He strives all people to deceive—
  This sturdy, bluff old ram,
But seeks to make his friends believe
  He's just a humble lamb.

Full soon—too soon—he'll reach the rim
  Where swift days fairly whiz;
A little child will walk with him—
  A little hand in his.

The Tides of Life! The Tides of Life!
  They rise and fall to bless:
To take away all grief and strife—
  And bring back happiness!

. . . . . .

Naylor's loving wife Lena Ervilla Naylor, stood by his side, ever
the helpmate, ever supportive. In their last years together, he
penned the lines below just for her. He did, indeed, leave
this world before her. Naylor died on April 4, 1945; she died
nearly eleven years later, on February 23, 1956.

When I Die

When the scenes of life are fading,
Shall I hold your hand in mine?
I could then brave every terror,
Press on to lands divine.

You would never leave me, darling,
To fight the fight alone?
My love I'll leave with you, dear,
Heart—whole—with you alone.

. . . . . .

The following poem was chosen for the title of Naylor's biography because it exemplifies his philosophy of life. Although he welcomed the acclaim he received, what ultimately mattered most to him were the people he loved and the joy and comfort he brought to others in his role as a physician.

The Final Test

When all is said and all is done,
      When all is lost or all is won—
In spite of musty theory,
      Of purblind faith and vain conceit,
Of barren creed and sophistry;
      In spite of all—success, defeat,
The Judge accords to worst and best,
      Impartially, this final test:

What has thou done with brawn and brain,
      To help the world to lose or gain
An onward step? Canst reckon one
      Unselfish, brave or noble deed,
That thou—nor counting cost!—hast done
      To help a brother's crying need?
Not what professed nor what believed—
      But what good thing hast thou achieved!

Yea! What attempted—what achieved?
　　Be not dismayed, be not deceived!
The tinsel bauble called success—
　　The dross of wealth, the gloss of fame!—
That men throw up their hands to bless,
　　Is but an empty breath—a name.
Far better is one word that slips
　　In blessing, from a beggar's lips!

I hold to this: The loftiest soul,
　　Of one great universal whole,
Is but a weak and meager part;
　　The lowliest, by impulse fired
To worthy act of brain or heart,
　　Is heaven-blessed and God-inspired!—
A bit of His most wondrous plan;
　　And each a clod—and each a man!

The chosen few! Prate not to me
　　Of consecrated sanctity;
Nor stifle me, nor hedge me round
　　` With puzzles algebraical,
To prove that this is holy ground—
　　'Tis simply pharisaical!
God's heart of love is deep and wide—
　　And each soul has a place inside.

When all is said and all is done—
        The battle lost, the battle won!—
In spite of ancient theory,
        Of purblind faith and fruitless quest,
Of threadbare creed and sophistry—
        In spite of all—this is the test:
What has thou done with brawn or brain,
        To help the world a step to gain!

. . . . . .

Writings of James Ball Naylor

Collected Verse

1893   *Current Coins Picked Up at a Country Railway Station*, S. Q. Lapius, Columbus, Ohio, Hann & Adair, Printers and Bookmakers.

1896   *Golden Rod and Thistle Down*, S. Q. Lapius, Columbus, Ohio., Hann & Adair, Printers and Bookmakers.

1906   *Old Home Week*, C. M. Clark Publishing Co., Boston, Mass.

1906-1907 *Old Home Week*, C. M. Clark Publishing Co., Boston, Mass. Governor Rollins Version, (double copyright).

1906-1907 *Old Home Week*, C. M. Clark Publishing Co., Boston, Mass. Mayor Fitzgerald Version, (double copyright).

1907   *Songs From the Heart of Things*, New Franklin Printing Company, Columbus, Ohio.

1927   *A Book of Buckeye Verse*, Tucker-Kenworthy Co. Press, Chicago, Ill.

1935   *Vagrant Verse, Morgan County Herald*, McConnelsville, Ohio.

1968   *A Second Book of Vagrant Verse*, Preface by Lucile Naylor, D. W. Garber. (One copy only).

Serialized Writings

1896-1897 "Beggars Awheel," *Ohio Farmer*, December 3, 1896 to January 21, 1897.

1897-1898 "In the Days of St. Clair," *Ohio State Journal*, December 5, 1897, to February 27, 1898.

1898-1899 "Under Mad Anthony's Banner," *Ohio State Journal*, November 27, 1898, to March 5, 1899.

1900-1901 "The Sign of the Prophet," *Ohio State Journal*, October 28, 1900, to February 10, 1901.

1904   "The Witch Crow and Barney Bylow," *National Magazine*, V. 21, No. 3, December, 1904 through V. 22, No. 1, April, 1905.

1905   "The Little Green Goblin of Goblinville," *National Magazine,* V. 22 and 23, September and October, 1905.

1906   "From Jim to Jack; Letters to an Old Time Schoolmate," *Ohio Magazine*, V. l, 1906.

1907-1908 "A Counterfeit Coin," *Ohio Magazine*, Columbus, Ohio, Vol. 3 and 4.

1926   "Physicians of Morgan County," *The Weekly Herald*, January 21, 1926 through March 4, 1926.

| 1927 | "Rambling Reminiscences," *Morgan County Herald*, McConnelsville, Ohio, March 29, 1927. |
| 1939 | "Straight Sticks from the Brush of Old Morgan County," *Morgan County Herald*, McConnelsville, Ohio, June 15, 1939 through September 7, 1939. |

Novels

1899	*Under Mad Anthony's Banner, Ohio State Journal,* Chauplin Press, Columbus, Ohio, 1899.
1901	*Ralph Marlowe*, Saalfi eld Publishing Co., Akron, Ohio.
1901	*The Sign of the Prophet*, Saalfi eld Publishing Co., Akron, Ohio.
1902	*In the Days of St. Clair*, Saalfi eld Publishing Co., Akron, Ohio.
1903	*Under Mad Anthony's Banner*, Saalfi eld Publishing Co., Akron, Ohio.
1904	*The Cabin in the Big Woods*, Saalfi eld Publishing Co., Akron, Ohio.
1905	The *Kentuckian*, C. M. Clark Publishing Co., Boston, Mass.
1907	*The Scalawags*, B. W. Dodge and Co., New York.
1908	The *Misadventures of Marjory*, C. M. Clark Publishing Co., Boston, Mass.

Children's Books

1906	*Witch Crow and Barney Bylow*, Saalfi eld Publishing Co., Akron, Ohio.
1907	*The Little Green Goblin*, Saalfi eld Publishing Co., Akron, Ohio.
1909	*Dicky Delightful in Rainbow Land*, Saalfi eld Publishing Co., Akron, Ohio.

Pamphlets

1907	*From Jim to Jack*, Herald Printing Co., McConnelsville, Ohio.
1911	*Across the Miles*, Rustcraft, Kansas City, Mo.
1911	*UCT Booklet*, United Commercial Travelers, Zanesville, Ohio.
1911	*Angelina's Ardent Lovers*, Advertising Poem.
1912	*For You*, Rustcraft, Kansas City, Mo.
1912	*If You Were Here*, Rustcraft Co., Kansas City, Mo.
1912	*The Old Time Friend*, Rustcraft Co., Kansas City, Mo.
1921	*Old Morgan County*, Poem, Herald Printing Co., McConnelsville, Ohio.
1921	*The Muskingum Valley*, Malta, Ohio, June, 1919.
1927	*Rambling Reminiscences*, Herald Printing Co., McConnelsville, Ohio.
--	*Flinch*, Advertising Poem.

Short Stories

| 1897 | "Ben's Adventure," S. Q. Lapius, Copyright 1897. |
| 1903 | "Ol' Cap Mingo," *National Magazine*, V. 17, No. 4, January, 1903. |

1903	"How Tom Evans Won his Wife," *National Magazine*, V. 17, No. 5, February, 1903.
1903	"The Mishaps of O1' Andy Perdue," *National Magazine*, V. 17, No. 6, March 1903.
1903	"A Lucky Opal," *National Magazine*, V. 18, No. 4, July, 1903.
1903	"Sim Spike's Misadventures," *National Magazine*, V. 19, October, 1903 (reference to)
1903	"The Youthful Indescretions of Jim Whiss," *National Magazine*, V. 19, October, 1903 Reference to *Ohio Star*, August, 1909.
1906	"The Undoing of Old John Chaney," *Ohio Magazine*, V. 4., 1906
--	"Coming of Sawlus," S. Q. Lapius.
--	"Did It Pay?," S. Q. Lapius.
--	"Jud Trainor's Ghost," *Ohio State Journal*.
--	"Mamie's Prisoner," *Ohio State Journal*.
--	"The Diversions of Dicky Dare."
--	"The Blackmer Affair," S. Q. Lapius.
--	"The Mills of the Gods," S. Q. Lapius.
--	"One of Morgan's Men," S. Q. Lapius
--	"Spike from the Underground Railway," S. Q. Lapius.
--	"Story of a Skeleton," S. Q. Lapius.
--	"Stuff of Which Doctors are Made," S. Q. Lapius.
--	"Two Consultations at Mam Sterlings," S. Q. Lapius.
--	"Wild Tom," S. Q. Lapius

Newspaper Columns

1913	*The Ohio Star*, Marion, Ohio.
1913	"Sunshine Corner," *The Marion Star*, Marion, Ohio.
1915-1923	"Life's Vaudeville," *The Marion Star*, Marion, Ohio.
1920-1923	*The Chicago Journal of Commerce*, Chicago, Illinois.
1925-1928	*The Week*.

Political Sketches (Who's You in Ohio)

--	Allen Oh! Meyers
--	An'-drew Lightning Harris
1907	Charles Hungry Grosvenor
1907	Elmer C. Dover
1907	George Boss Cox
1907	Jon'ah McLean
1907	Joseph Beensome Foraker
1907	Kernel William Alexander Taylor
1907	May-Jar Charles Dick
--	Nickle-Us Longworth
1907	Theodore Energy Burton

| 1907 | Tom Lofty Johnson |
| 1907 | William How-Hard Taft |

Campaign Songs

| 1920 | Republican Campaign Songs, Ohio Republican State Executive Committee, Columbus, Ohio. |

Presented in Programs

1904	A Voice from the Past
1904	Down Upon the Rappahannock
1904	Flinch
1904	Follerin' the Fife and Drum
1904	My Skies are Seldom Gray
1904	The Fifer of the Buck Run Band
1904	The Girl Who Sings Popular Songs
1904	The Ol' Country Dance
1904	The Physical Culture Fad
1904	The Song in My Heart
1908	Foolin' Ma
1908	Song of the Motor Car
1908	The Cumberland Stage
1917	Old Glory, April 19, 1917
1917	Some Singers, June 4, 1917
1923	Minor American Singers, August 20, 1923
--	Boyhood Days
--	One Country, One People, One Flag
--	Pop Goes the Weasel
	Snip, A Study of a Boy and his Dog
	The Diversions of Dicky Dare
	The Jester
	The Millionaire Dude
	When You and I Were Boys
	Whistling Jimmy

Christmas Cards

Christmas in the Heart
From a Friend in Old Morgan County
Good Luck to You
Holiday Greetings
The Home Light
The Old Home Place

Broadsides

Bully Yankee
Call Him, Can Him and Cuss Him
Dr. John Goodfellow--Office Upstairs
Foolin' Ma
Gallery of the Immortals
Hands Across the Sea
My Laddie's Life Lesson
The One Flag
To Her Who Keeps My Dwelling Place
Ye Doctor's Life
Yours and Mine
What America Means

Unpublished Material

1908	Castle of Doors and Shutters, Children's story.
	The Fate of the Valley Belle, (A Barefoot Avenger), Story.
	Two Men and a Boy, Story.
	The Adventures of the Elephant, the Monkey and the Clown, Poem.
	The Cowboy and the Doctor, Comedy Sketch.
	Two of a Kind, Comedy Sketch.
1916	The Little Town of Toddville, Play.
	The Jackies, Play.
	One Country, Entertainment Program.
	When You and I Were Boys, Entertainment Program.

INDEX

INDEX

INDEX

INDEX

The Final Test
A Biography of James Ball Naylor

by
Theresa Marie Flaherty

www.JamesBallNaylor.com

CPSIA information can be obtained at www.ICGtesting.com
262579BV00001BA/2/P